DEDICATION

This book is dedicated to the memory of my mother and my sister, who both meant the world to me and who inspired me to become better.

I also write this book in dedication to other women who have suffered through difficult circumstances; to give them the courage and power to move past these difficulties and find their path.

DISCLAIMER

Although the events that I relate in this volume are factual, the names of persons mentioned throughout the book have been changed in order to protect their privacy.

THINGS THAT WERE LEFT UNSAID SPILLED out, like the remnants of a once-overflowing basket filled with rotten vegetables. They were the spoils of youth meant to be carefree and vibrant, but that had instead turned sour.

"We're moving!" my father announced.

It was a defining moment that changed everything for me, as a child. We were not allowed to question, although deep down I knew the answer.

"But Daddy, it's not fair!" not daring to defy him, yet wanting to express my own opinion.

"What are you waiting for?" he bellowed. "Snap to it! We need to get out... RIGHT NOW!"

As the tears leaked uncontrollably out of the corners of my eyes, I pleaded; "What about school? I have school tomorrow, Daddy."

"There will be no more school. Now do as I say!" he yelled, standing over me with his commanding presence.

Despite the protests of my mother and unknowing angst

of my baby sister, we packed up everything we owned in less than two hours. My father had lost the house to loan sharks when I was only eight. We were ordered to leave.

Why had he done this, we wondered. In haste, I gathered only what would fit within a satchel. Two mid-knee length tattered dresses, a pair of sandals I had outgrown, a special 'star' sticker from my best friend, Tunne and a blue ribbon for winning a first prize in singing at the State Fair was all I could grab.

Our family was very poor. We came from Loeng Nok Tha, Thailand, which is a district named after a swampy basin of low-lying land as well as a specific Thai bird that is now nearly extinct. The district was mostly comprised of farmland, of which we happened to be part of.

Although our family were farmers by trade, we were the poorest folks in the entire community. We have my father, Tong Suku to thank for that. Although he came from an affluent heritage, my father's alcohol and gambling addictions always took precedence over his own family's well-being. Some of his ruthless friends were a bad influence, often stealing his time for card games, drinking binges and brothels. Hence the bad luck followed us, like black soot that has fallen to the ground after a great fire.

However, my father was more than just a black sheep. He had become the embarrassment of the family's honor. Disgrace was something always frowned upon, no matter what country your native of origin.

THE QUEST FOR SERENDIPITY

My grandparents were very wealthy. They owned a successful farm in Mongolia, however because of my father's behavior he had been stamped out of their will. Upon their passing, the inheritance had still been divided equally amongst all of their children, including my father.

Instead of using his inheritance for good measures and bettering his family, my father lost most of the money within a short time span. Drinking, gambling and reckless partying were the fuel that burned his money up in flames. He also lost his carpentry and teaching jobs due to his foolish behavior. Sometimes he was so hung over he could not get out of bed. A couple of days would pass after a heavy nights of partying.

Since I was only three years old when my father's parents died, I barely remember my grandparents except as very kind people who were quite tall. I was too young to know any better about my father's haphazard gambling expeditions, except for the ensuing fights between him and my Mom.

Whenever the fights escalated, my sister and I were forced to leave the room. Penny was just a toddler. Sometimes my concern for my mother and childhood curiosity got the better of me as I peeked cautiously around the corner, just in time to see my drunken father slap my mother across the face or pin her down until she cried for mercy. This happened on more than one occasion.

Alas, these decisions were the preclusion to our life of deserved wealth, versus the reality of poverty and struggle.

To say that we were the very poorest family within our community is not very far from the truth, by my account.

Looking back, it did not have to be this way. My father came from a highly educated background and was in the military. He was very handsome and stood tall at 6'2". His dark complexion and signature facial freckles were deemed the beauty marks of a Mongolian countenance.

While serving in Thailand for military duty he met my mother, fell in love and got married. Standing only at five feet in height, my mother was a hot little spitfire next to my Dad. The two made a cute couple. I know they really did love each other because my mother stayed by his side. I think she always held on to that glimmer of hope that my father would give up his bad habits and become the better father and husband she always longed for him to be.

My parents had three children prior to me and my younger sister. I never knew my older siblings well because they had already moved out on their own to create new families and lives. The other kids had left town by the time I was still a toddler. Most likely, they had moved as far away as possible to escape the atmosphere of my father's irresponsible ways and the shame we faced by others who lived in our community.

My eldest brother was 15 when I was born. He had lived within the city and gone to college to further his education. It was something I'm sure my mother was proud of, although we rarely saw or heard from him again after he was old enough to escape. My older sisters had gotten married and moved elsewhere. My parents rarely spoke of them, but my hunch was that the unacceptable family patterns and my father had driven them as far away as possible. From what I later learned, my family was not always poor. When my older brother and sisters were much younger, my father had actually worked respectfully as a carpenter and provided for his family rather well. They were considered middle-class at that time.

It was after his parents passed away and my father blew his inheritance that karma kicked him back with a fierce retribution. That karma boot was a real bitch. Unfortunately it affected all of us, not just my Dad.

From what I was told, my father was also once a prominent member of the community as a respected teacher, after his carpentry job expired. However, upon arriving at the school one day profusely sweating and smelling like moonshine the school fired him. "This is not the example we wish to present to our students," said the head school advisor as he let him go.

By the time I was a very young girl, our circumstances were quite severe. I never knew what it was like to be middle class, except in my daydreams when I imagined wearing silk blouses and fashionable jewelry like the movie stars.

Yet, strange as it seemed, I did not see my Dad as a bad man. As a father, he was generally a caring person who would have given anyone his last penny, despite being poor. However, his biggest downfall were drinking and gambling addictions. Those two evil spirits haunted him, even if it meant sacrificing the well-being of his own family.

I don't think he meant to lose the house and hurt us like he did. His intentions were to borrow money from the loan shark in order to support our family. The loan backfired. He was unable to repay the money by the deadline and had used our home as collateral.

I overheard my Dad telling my mother right before we packed that these guys were ruthless. The loan sharks had recently gone to the home of another man my father knew from poker nights and dragged him out of bed, blindfolded him, and beat him up in the yard until he could no longer see. While this was happening his wife ran outside screaming so the men kicked her too. They ordered the man to repay the money by the next day at noon or they would take their lives. The man offered these evil lenders everything he owned, including a small chicken farm that was worth more than the loan. The loan sharks did not accept his offer and instead killed his wife the next day, when the family did not meet their obligations. They tied her to the back of a small pickup truck and dragged her helplessly for miles.

As the dust settled upon her lifeless body, it was hard to distinguish whether she was a man or a woman. Blood-soaked, tattered clothes left a trail from their home to a nearby gravel pit. That was where they threw her body. She was worth nothing more to them than a pair of old shoes or stale lettuce from an uneaten sandwich. To these coldblooded hunters, a human life was far less valuable than even a few hundred dollars borrowed with for lost regrets.

That is why we left in such a hurry.

Apparently our destination was to be the Cambodian border on the far outskirts of Thailand, far away from any civilization. My father had staked a claim of unchartered land there and his goal was to turn the land and farm it to earn enough money to buy the house back. Back in those days there was still plenty of land available to those who were brave enough or desperate enough to plot it. Unlike the early frontiersmen of America, the people who claimed land in Thailand could expect a jungle full of willowy trees and poisonous insects. For me, moving to this this overgrown region was nothing to be excited about.

My father reassured my mother that our newly claimed plot of land would be the answer to repay the loan sharks. And so we began our journey in the hot sun. He rambled on about all of the ideas he had to harvest the land. My mother was clearly perturbed and angry, as her furrowed forehead revealed. She hardly said a word, yet her thoughts could be heard through silent flames of pensive disgust.

I didn't know how long it would take, but the painful trek had just begun. Distance always seems like days when you're a child. Especially when you're walking in the humid air and sticky heat.

That day I left any sense of childhood joy behind. There was no room for it in my satchel and my father would not have allowed it to be brought along anyhow. We were not allowed to have an opinion about moving. We were expected to follow orders and go along with what we were told to do.

The four of us packed like hobos, with knapsacks full of broken promises and unfulfilled pleasures. With our few worldly possessions and just each other, we left our home in Loeng Nok Tha behind as we trod to a land unknown and unwanted.

Chapter

2

MY MOTHER LIFTED MY SISTER AND ME over the rushing waters of the Mekong River. Holding one child by the hand and the other by the waist for dear life, she clung with the strength of an eagle as it wraps its talons around something precious. The strong current ran angrily around us, almost as if it were pushing us to leave town. The river spilled its rage upon our innocence. Its lashing ripples swirled around me like a whirlpool of anger, just daring me to make one false move.

Yet we trudged on, soaked and undefeated. I clung to my mother's hand for dear life. This river commanded the utmost of respect, with its angry union against the ferns of the eastern banks. Its fearful rage devoured the weak in spirit and strength. My mother would have drowned herself before allowing her children to be pulled away by the river's strength. Her will was stronger than the current, but one false move and all three of us could have easily been sucked in.

After we crossed the river's white-tipped fingers that deceivingly beckoned us to come under and be swept away, all of us were soaked and shaken. We looked like wet cats that had been thrown into the water for the first time, with matted hair and arched backs. Nevertheless, we made it. Crossing the Mekong represented a new life, one that we had not chosen and would be forced to accept.

My father made a small fire and our family sat huddled around it in silence; even my baby sister. The fire was tantalizing, mesmerizing and crackled high into the night sky. Our lives were about to change dramatically, as our new existence as gypsies began. We were quiet. Once again, Mom saved us from a dire situation.

In fact, if it weren't for my mother I would not be here right now. She was the strong beam who held my family together as well as the bright beacon who kept our spirits high, even when we had absolutely nothing. Oh yes, there were those times. She was everything you could ask for in a mother... affectionate, caring, beautiful and very intelligent. If we had one fish to eat and nothing else, my mother would give it to her children before she ever took so much as one nibble. She only ate if there was a morsel leftover. My mother was very nurturing, funny and warm. Every day, no matter how poor we were, my mother always told my sister and I how much she loved us.

My mother's love kept me going and established the ambitious nature within me that I still hold present to this day.

She was also very good at business. It came naturally to

her, just as a writer to a pen or a painter to a brush. Her God-given talent was an aptitude for making money, which at the time was not so common for a woman in Thailand. My mother had a knack for making nothing worth something and for seeing the invisible become tangible. This was a gift and a quality that saved our family time and time again.

Let me explain. My mother came from a farming background. Although I never met my grandparents on her side of the family because they passed away before I was born, there were some skills she had learned along the way that became an asset to our plight. She taught my sister and me how to grow food, harvest and then sell it. She was a hustler and was not shy about getting top dollar for her products. My mother could turn one simple cucumber into a dinner for our entire family for two evenings. Her business savvy was something I kept a close eye on and picked up a knack for eventually.

We dressed up to go to the market some days, which consisted of wearing the only outfit left that was not dirty from digging in the garden. Our family was so poor that we did not have shoes to wear to school, so we walked everywhere barefoot. The earth from the marshy hills of Thailand often squished between our toes, especially during the rainy seasons. Let's just say that we did not always make a favorable impression because of our appearance. It was only because of having street smarts that enabled us to survive amongst the harsh days of living on nothing more than a sense of faith.

Sometimes we were unable to sell anything or barter. It was those times that we simply asked for what we needed. I lived on borrowed dreams during those days. In my mind, I did not perceive myself to be the poor peasant girl, but instead a girl who was rich, famous and successful.

My mother sent me to the temple every morning before school. Using her keen sense of business savvy, I devised a way in which to transport water from the temple with me to the school. The school kids all wanted fresh water and my water was the cleanest, most refreshing-tasting water to be found. None of them knew that it came from the Temple, but it sure tasted holy.

Sometimes I sold the water, whereas other times I traded it for tomatoes, rice or a cucumber to feed my family. If I happened to find the right child to barter with, I could sometimes even get meat or eggs. Anytime I made money or food outside of the home, I brought back the earnings to benefit my family.

Since she was so resourceful, my mother could make our food stretch for days when she needed to. She was such a smart business lady with a sharp entrepreneurial spirit. Had she been born in another place and era, I have no doubt that my mother could have honed in on her natural talent for business and perhaps been a very wealthy woman. Regrettably, she had married my father instead. And as the saying goes; "A fool and his money are soon parted." This was true in my father's case.

We were taught to work from as early as I can remember.

THE QUEST FOR SERENDIPITY

It was not a chore for children to work in Thailand as it is here in America. Working was an expectation and requirement just as much as living was a privilege.

When there was no work, my sister and I were sent by my parents to knock on doors and ask for jobs to earn money. Beggars we were not. There were many odd jobs we did to earn money, from cleaning up after farm animals to carrying buckets filled with papayas; or digging holes or even sewing clothes and blankets. My mother brought me with her to the market when we did have money. It was there I learned by watching my mother's uncanny knack for doing business and the hustling she did to swap vegetables for meat and eggs for seed. I wanted to become ambitious, too.

Everything my mother did was for me and my sister. She lived for us and for the joy of making us happy. Instead of ever telling us we could not do something, my Mom always encouraged us to strive for a better life.

My deep desire to be wealthy and successful came at an early age. It was not because we were poor, rather a longing that I had within my soul. I dreamed of being discovered as a famous singer or actress and taking my rightly spot on the big stage. I could even hear the loud clap of an audience in the background in my imagination. They were cheering just for me.

Sadly, there was no clapping now. We were moving away from the one chance I had left to be discovered and become famous.

As I stared pensively at the fire, I thought of all the times my mother had taken me to the State Fairs specifically to enter the singing contests. People told me I was pretty, having sweet freckles and skin coloring from my Mongolian father; blended fascinatingly with the curvy lips and long lashes from my beautiful Thai mother. Singing was one of the few joys I remember experiencing as a child.

We bartered vegetables or fruit in exchange for fabric to make a nice dress for the singing contests so that I could look fabulous in a great debut. When I was up on stage I felt peaceful, happy and alive. I felt like a superstar. My mother was always in the first row of the audience; she was my biggest fan and supporter. Being on stage and admired even for a few moments was a magnificent feeling since the rest of my childhood was not so fortunate.

Now as the four of us sat huddled around the fire, the only stars to be seen were those twinkling down at us from the black sky. My Dad tried to lighten the mood by telling a story or two. Silently, I held my jaw down in resentment.

"It'll be fun being gypsies," he said. "We get to travel around and see the countryside."

I didn't speak.

"We can live off the land with no worries and no one to bother us. A little peace and quiet never hurt anyone," he said. We all listened but didn't want to hear him.

I had seen gypsies before at the State Fair. My mother had taken me there each year to sing and I saw them with their scraggly hair and earthen appearance. The gypsies worked for the State Fair and traveled with it to every district within Thailand. They roamed in caravels with run-down trailers and some of the gypsies dressed like hobos.

Most of them were friendly enough. They smiled at the children with gummed lips and wrinkled frows. They were free-spirited and unpretentious.

Yet somehow, the gypsies always made me feel a tiny bit better about the fact that we were poor, because at least we had a roof over our heads. Even though our house was slightly run down, it offered that one piece of stability. It was a place to go. Once you have no place to go, life is a lot different.

When you're a child, a home is the one comfort you have. A special pillow or a raggedy quilt provides that one shred of dignity to make you feel covered in warmth, instead of being out in the open.

So when we moved, we left our dignity behind. I lost my opportunity for education because there were no schools in the middle of the jungle. I was unable to finish high school until later on in life. My dreams were left behind, at least for the time being. The next few years were to be all about work.

Ultimately, by the time I finally began earning the respect of the other students was the same time that we were abruptly told to leave our home. I was on the honor roll, had a couple of good female friends, a cute boyfriend and was finally making decent money for my family. For about a year I was happy, although we were still poor. The only times I was not so happy was when my father came home early, particularly after he lost his job and stayed home hung over from a two-day bender every three or four days. I was much happier outside of my home than I was while there, although I did enjoy my mother's company immensely.

As we rolled over on the hard ground by the river banks of the Mekong, I curled up next to my mother and baby sister. I stared into the darkness wondering what the next few days would bring. I wondered if I would ever see my friends again. I wondered if I would ever get to sing or be on stage. I wondered if the loan sharks were going to come after us. Would they kill us? Would they find us? These thoughts ran through my head as I was unable to get comfortable on the hard surface.

Wrapped up in my mother's arms to keep warm, I did feel somewhat safe despite the lack of shelter. Her soft bosoms were like cushy pillows for a child's head. "Goodnight, Mommy," I whispered.

"Goodnight, sweet Nuensie. I love you," she whispered back. Finally, I drifted off in exhaustion.

Chapter

3

THE MOST COLORFUL THING I REMEMBER about the place where I was raised was the temple that we attended and worshipped at. Although the temple was as old as the city itself, it was a massive palace both inside and out. It was decorated extravagantly in vivid colors of gold, yellow, orange and red. The temple was luxuriously appointed as our dwelling of solace. Visiting this place of worship near daily was the sparkle in my innocent eyes, providing a comforting and sensually inviting atmosphere.

I found myself daydreaming as we worshipped, like children do. My mind often wandered ahead to the future, one with brick pathways that paved the way in gold shades of clay. The way to prosperity and wealth. Spirituality was a big part of my childhood. Without it I would not be where I am today. It was this feeling beyond reality that offered me inspiration.

The people of my town considered the temple to be very sacred. There were two statues of Buddha, one sculpted in heavy rock and another more modern version of steel. We gave thanks to Buddha and prayed to him. In my imagination my prayers were answered. I prayed to be rich, to have a better life and to be the very best at everything I did. I prayed to become a celebrity one day and to see my name on the big screen at the movie theatre, or to hear my voice on the radio.

My family was so poor that we only had an old portable radio that my father had resurrected from a local junk yard. It was rigged to intercept a few channels if you set the radio somewhere near an open window. It only worked on days that were not too foggy. On the days that we were able to listen, I could hear singers from the opera or the soft songs channel. Those were the moments that I often fantasized of becoming famous.

Everyone believed and was taught to meditate and pray not just once a week, but every day. We were taught that if we gave food to the temple or money and riches that those very amenities would be waiting for us in the afterlife. If we gave food there would be food waiting. If we gave belongings – such as jewelry or valuables – those material possessions would be waiting for us on the other side. If we gave money there would be an entire temple waiting for us. That was our belief. Whatever we gave we would receive tenfold. This is one principle that I still hold steadfast to this day with firm belief.

Throughout the difficult years, I never let on to other people that my family was poor. Of course, the other children knew that we were. There were whispers among the rich kids.

THE QUEST FOR SERENDIPITY

Some students wouldn't walk with me because I was poor and they were ashamed for me. Others were just too embarrassed to associate with someone of my stature, so they just ignored me. It was not that I was disliked by my classmates; rather I was a misfit marked by the overachieving middle to upper class.

The burning desire to be successful stayed with me every moment and I never gave up on that dream. Instead of hanging my head in shame for living with less than others, I used my talents to surround myself with those whom I most admired. Those few friends I had were more affluent than I was. I chose not to hang out with the other poor kids because they represented a lifestyle I did not want for myself. By associating with wealth, I was certain to attract wealth. Some were children of parents who had obtained a higher education or who were business owners. I too, dreamed of becoming a business owner.

Although I wore rags to school that were made to look fancier by an adornment of a sash or scarf, I carried myself with poise. I studied furiously and knew that my ticket to becoming famous or owning a business one day was to be very smart. Thankfully, the great Universe bestowed upon me the same intellect that was inherent of my mother. I saw this natural blessing as an opportunity to achieve more.

The schools we attended were not like those you might expect in a standard classroom. There was no blackboard, chalk or erasers. There were no books. We wrote everything down that was required by our teacher and then reused it daily after thoroughly wiping it down with rubbing alcohol. I remembered everything I learned, like a human computer. I passed tests in half the time allotted and was always the first to answer difficult equations or literature citations.

The other students took notice of my knowledge and gained a quiet respect for my intelligence. As we all crowded around on the floor, sitting cross-legged on small rugs crafted of hemp and twine, the other students began to admire me for my audacious answers and unbridled imagination. There was less ridicule among peers when I was on the honor roll. Admittedly, I kind of enjoyed school. Not just for the social aspect, but also for the chance to stimulate the longing for achievement. It also offered a reprieve from the situation at home. When I was at school I didn't have to listen to my parents argue.

In order to ensure that our friendships were mutually beneficial, I helped the other children with their studies. Being wealthy was not a guarantee of brilliance. A few students began asking me for favors to improve their grades. Namely, homework assignments or tutoring. This was how I met two of my best childhood friends, Tunne and Farra.

Tunne's family was well off. They owned the biggest general store in town. Everyone shopped there for common household necessities, making their last name synonymous with provisions for Loeng Nok Tha. They had money, and lots of it. Tunne was not a showoff but she was someone that others gravitated to because of her outward beauty. Her raven black hair and pretty teeth were the perfect accent to a beautiful wardrobe of well-made fabric dresses that were worn by the affluent folk. People might say she had stunning beauty, like a rare bird on an exotic Polynesian island.

And Farra was a farm girl, much like me. Her parents were also rich from having a successful chicken and rice farm. They were one of the few families within the city to have a couple of servants. Although Farra did not dress as chic as Tunne, she did not go without and most certainly would never have been caught dead wearing peasant's clothing. Lucky for me, both girls were not good at studying. In fact they were not good at doing homework or schoolwork of any kind. Nor did they have any desire to be. One of them was flunking math, while the other risked repeating a grade to make up for too many failing marks.

In Thailand, there is no policy similar to the *"No kid left behind"* policy, such as there is in the U.S. It was Farra who first approached me with a generous bag of eggs.

"There's more where this came from," she said as she carefully set the bag of eggs in my lap one random day. I had just sat down for the morning school session.

As I looked up, Farra smiled down and proposed the idea of a mutually beneficial friendship. I happily agreed. Hence, I was expected to help her with her homework and guarantee her passing on to the next grade. In return, she brought me a variety of foods, including mushrooms, rice or meat that I always gave to my family. We made this arrangement not just because my family needed food, but also because I wanted a friend.

It was at this point I realized the value of friendship. Friendship is give and take. Finding a mutually beneficial point to unite and then making an exchange to meet the needs of each other is a great concept. More friends should do this.

Tunne was also a friend of Farra's. They must have talked because she also proposed a similar arrangement of friendship. Like Farra, Tunne also brought me many useful tokens from her family's general store. Every item – from a bar of soap to a particular herb for cooking – was at her disposal. These efforts helped my family a great deal. What's more, Tunne's mesmerizing personality was enjoyable. I never felt used by either of the two girls' friendships. However, I did realize the main reasons they had befriended me.

Over time, Tunne became the lasting friend out of the two girls. In fact, we still keep in touch with each other to this very day. I do still hear from Tunne once in a blue moon. Every couple of years we either exchange cards or letters, or one of us makes a call to the other. A friendship that began as one hand washing the other eventually blossomed into a friendship for life.

Back then, the best qualities about Tunne and Farra (by my standards) were that the two girls never looked down upon me, especially after we all became acquainted. After only a brief spell of hanging out together, they realized that poverty did not make me a bad person. Tunne and Farra inspired me and even protected me when I was taunted by other students. Both friends were positive influences whom I admired. Listening to their stories, I was able to learn much about the day-to-day happenings of managing or owning a business.

Together, the three of us often schemed of new ideas to make money. We were the young lady entrepreneurs, yet none of us were over the age of ten! I dreamed that one day I would have my own business and live in a palace, one that was just as divine as the gorgeous temple of worship.

Between studying, schooling, worshipping and selling things with my friends and doing their homework, there was very little time left for me. I also helped my parents with work and with raising my baby sister, Penny. Therefore, I didn't have time to truly enjoy my childhood. Much of it was a blur.

My true childhood mentor was neither Tunne nor Farra. A young boy named Duey was my dearest friend of all. He lived nearby, within walking distance to my parent's home. I sensed he felt badly for me, as he saw me walking to the temple and school every day. I carried as much water from the temple to the school as I could. Walking barefoot with an armload of water is not an easy feat for a seven year old, yet I was strong physically and had the determination of an Olympic athlete.

"Can I help you carry that water?" Duey asked me one day.

I nodded and handed him an armload. "Thank you," I replied. The boy was kind of cute. He was Japanese which made him different than the other boys at school. His dark brown hair was clean cut with long bangs. His eyes were different and his face was heart shaped, giving him a boyish, yet young manly sort of look. Duey wore nice clothes in the native Japanese fashion, making him distinctively handsome among the normal things worn by young Thai males.

The day he first offered to help me, I remember he wore red. To me, red seemed like a royal color. It was always a color I have been drawn to, perhaps from the lovely red colors of the temple. As we walked and talked I got to know him better. He spoke fluent Thai and Japanese. He was also learning Chinese. Duey was intelligent, yet reverent. He was not judgmental.

Although he had lived in Thailand for the majority of his childhood, Duey was born in Japan. His parents immigrated to the city and had built a grand hardware store to serve the town. I never knew the reason why they chose Thailand – specifically Loeng Nok Tha – to make their home, but I sensed that maybe his parents had fled Japan on bad terms.

Nevertheless, Duey's family had become one of the wealthiest within our community. We made it a daily ritual to walk together. Secretly, there was a bit of chemistry between us. We had a crush on each other, yet our young ages made it too forbidden to pursue. Duey was definitely my first girlhood crush, but he was also my very best friend.

THE QUEST FOR SERENDIPITY

Duey became an instrumental mentor to me when I told him about all of the many different ways I had learned to make money for my family. Homework assistance, farming, selling water from the temple and trading eggs or vegetables at the market had been working successfully for me. Duey also taught me many more ways to make money, without toiling or breaking so much as one bead of sweat.

I guess you could say he was my boyfriend. His parents liked me, too. Often they welcomed me to their beautiful home to share a meal with them. Their house was well-kept, with fancy ceramic tile imported from Japan. They used beaded curtains to set apart each room, but the grand room for entertaining was very spacious and open. The beads were so lovely I could have worn them as jewelry. Duey's mother had a flair for decorating and had adorned their walls with very ornate artwork and sculptures. Their home emitted a welcoming atmosphere with lush vegetation and bonsai trees. One day, this was exactly the type of home I hoped to own.

Duey often gave me little things from his parent's general store that I could then sell. There were multi-colored rubber bands that his father got for free in the shipping materials. Duey gathered them all and presented them one day in a small sack, such as one would find for packaging.

My eyes lit up like the sparkle of the first fireworks. To me, these rubber bands represented a new opportunity. It was almost like getting a fist full of cash. We made up a game that could be played with the rubber bands and small stones. On the school grounds kids gathered around as we played the game nonchalantly. They all wanted to know where to find these rubber bands. Of course the only avenue was through me and Duey. I charged them all the equivalent of an American dollar for each rubber band. The rubber bands were thick, so I knew each band would last long enough for playing. Everyone wanted them and those rubber bands were one of my hottest commodities to date.

Then a funny thing happened. Some of the cooler kids also began wearing the rubber bands around their wrists. I began selling them as wristbands. They were the fashion fad of the decade. Even kids who did not attend our school wanted them. It was then I realized how easy and resourceful it was to turn a free, simple gadget into an entrepreneurial idea. Of course, back then we just called it a business.

Things were going well for me once I finally made these friends. School, selling and my friends became my passion. They were my escape from the reality of home and the poverty we lived in. They were also my source of happiness as a child.

Alas, these three things all came to an abrupt and unexpected end the day my father announced our new plans. It was hard to accept and even more difficult to acknowledge. We left in such a hurry and were ordered to pack only what we could fit within a knapsack. I wondered what my friends would do without me or if they would miss me.

THE QUEST FOR SERENDIPITY

I left them all without even a chance to say goodbye. My childhood was not mine and never was. That was the sad and cruel reality of what was to become an even more unbearable existence.

Chapter

4

THE FIRST TIME YOU'VE EVER TAKEN A
bite from a little creature in the forest, it seems a bit
weird. Our family had to eat squirrels, frogs or mice
for meat. Of course we cooked them first, but the taste was
quite unusual. Squirrel stew has a fusty taste, like eating
shoes. Dry and leathery.

My family sauntered on as we came upon a farmhouse. It
was near the treacherous terrain of the Cambodian border.
We had been walking for three days now, spending nights
under the black skies and mysterious noises. The foliage was
thick and the population was sparse.

To come up on a farmhouse was to find other humans.
My father knocked on the door of the main house, but no
one answered. We saw a big gray barn made of stone, with
livestock, grain and a hayloft in the top half. The hay was
itchy, but comfortable as we all lay in there to wait. It was
raining and we were just thankful not to be walking in the
rain anymore. I think we were all so exhausted that we fell
asleep.

THE QUEST FOR SERENDIPITY

We awoke to the sound of boots clacking on the stone floor. The sound of bullets being loaded into a gun made us all sit up in fear and silence as we rose from our slumber at the same time. My mother placed her finger on her lips to hush my sister and me. We froze.

"I know someone is in here!" yelled a gruff voice. "The barn door is open. And it doesn't open by itself!"

Wide-eyed, we all stifled any movement and a tear rolled down the cheek of my baby sister.

The clacking of the boots got closer. Breaking the silence, my father spoke first. "Please, mister. Don't hurt us. We just walked all the way from Loeng Nok Tha for many days and we needed to rest. I am Thong. It is just me and my wife and two little daughters. I knocked on your door but there was no answer."

"Stand up so that I may see you!" the man bellowed.

My father cautiously stood up, with his hands raised up in the air. He faced the farmer, who was an elderly man with a graying beard. The farmer lowered his gun. My father stood a full foot taller than the man, who was very small but stout.

"We will leave," offered my Dad.

"Lemme see the rest of you," the man pointed.

Carefully, my mother then stood up holding my little sister, Penny. I was a little hesitant, but I stood up also. I'm sure we looked a little tired and bedraggled.

"Are you Thai or Cambodian?" asked the farmer.

"Thai," replied my Dad with a gulp. He had a fifty / fifty

chance of telling the farmer the answer he wanted to hear. We all held our breath in anticipation.

"Come on inside," said the farmer. "My wife will fix ya something to eat."

As we crowded around the farmhouse table with the farmer and his wife, we enjoyed the first good meal any of us had eaten in weeks. His wife made rice, chicken and cornbread; some of the best cornbread I've ever had. There were papayas for dessert, drenched in heavy whipped milk and brown sugar.

Without telling him about the whole story, my father explained that we had lost our home and that we were on a journey to the Southern border. The farmer offered our family a temporary job. "The harvest season is upon us," he explained. "I could use some helpers to pick and shuck the corn and rice."

Happily, our family agreed and the farmhouse was to become the first stop along our journey as gypsies. The farmer set aside one of the stalls to make a shelter for us. There was plenty of straw and musty blankets. We made a makeshift table out of a bale of hay. We weren't there much, except to sleep. The sun beat down upon us daily as we worked very hard; from sunup to sundown. There was no time for academics, only work.

If I wasn't in the harvest I was taking care of Penny. She too had to work even though she was very little. After she got tired, I took over the duties of her care while my mom and dad stayed very late in the fields. The days were long, yet the time we were there passed quickly.

We moved on after the corn and rice were harvested. My parents used some of the money to buy a tent and supplies at a nearby village that were recommended by the farmer. They bid us farewell and my mother exchanged hugs and a respectful bow to the farmer's wife, whom she had become friends with.

The farmer warned us not to go into Cambodia because the border wars were still undergoing. The Thai borders had not yet been clearly defined, and that is why there was still much unclaimed land along the outskirts. Most of the dispute centered around the Preah Vihear Temple, which was located on the border between Thailand and Cambodia high up in the majestic Dangrek Mountains. Overlooking both countries from its prominent spot atop the highest cliff, the eleventh-century old temple had never been demarcated, so both Thailand and Cambodia had staked their claim on the territory. The ancient temple was subsequently awarded to Cambodia in 1962, although the only accessible passage to get in or out was through Thailand.

A civil war even broke out over this very temple in 1970 and to this day there continues to be bloodshed between the Thai army and Cambodia. It has been very dangerous for at least a century.

There were other political disturbances between the two countries. These events occurred around the same time as tensions rose throughout Southeast Asia over the fear of communist expansion; leading to the war between Vietnam and the US. Although as children we remained mostly unaware of the reasons or the events that precluded these disturbances, we were privy to the fact that there was much hatred all around. We were scared of the military men, especially non-Thai military.

We had seen American soldiers in the city. To us, they were scary and big compared to the men of Thai descent. We were also a bit fearful of Cambodians, although at least they were mostly scouting for soldiers and not for civilians. Unless you happened to get in their way then it was safe to pass.

Frontiersmen still claimed land in Thailand that was unchartered. So, for anyone who had the nerve to do so, it was theirs for the taking. I'm not sure how my father knew where to go or which land had yet to be claimed. But once we were there, he knowingly set everything down. "Here we are," he stated.

My mom, sister and I looked at each other, as if expecting something more. It was just a thick forest on a ridge with a big overgrown field nearby. Lush foliage in the middle of the Thai jungle. We set up a tent and built a fire. For the next two years, this was to be our "home".

My sister and I were not allowed to stray anywhere. All we did was work, work, work. There were many opportunities to make money by working the land we had.

We made a garden and grew vegetables ourselves. There

were tomatoes, cucumbers, zucchini and onions. Mushrooms and herbs from the forest were there also. All of these were valuable assets that we took to the villages to sell. We learned which plants had value and which ones were poisonous. There were many creatures in the woods that we had to be wary of. Poisonous snakes, giant centipedes and caterpillars, fiery ants, wild dogs and even monkeys that could be dangerous. Quietness became a great comfort.

Being one with nature gave me ample time for dreaming. I still longed to become a famous entertainer. At times I imagined I was a slave who was rescued one day by a handsome prince. The prince whisked me away to a fairytale land of snow. Although I had never actually seen snow before, somehow I knew what it looked like in my dreams. It was white and fluffy and wonderful, like pillows or clouds.

Every morning my sister and I walked four or five miles to get water from a clear spring stream in the lowlands. We brought enough back for the family to use for the whole day. This became a ritual. Our rustic farm was just on the outskirts of the mountains, but it was high enough to avoid the flash flooding of the monsoon rains when they came.

My mother still taught me a lot about business, even though we lived in the middle of nowhere. There were no kids, no friends, no schools, and no people. The area was sparsely populated so those who did live nearby were still quite a fair distance between each other. We met most everyone within a thirty mile radius of our land. My mother taught us how to go door-to-door selling the vegetables and other products from the woods. She cooked the corn we harvested by boiling it and then panned it on the grill to sell. My sister and I walked to every farm selling the corn, mushrooms and a variety of other things. I swear my mother could have sold grass to a sand porpoise; she was that clever.

Our family also cut down timber from the woods and sold it. We found ways to sell every piece of the trees – from the bark to the roots for cooking and healing – to the stumps and branches for firewood and building. People came to know us and look forward to our products.

None of us were very happy. It was very difficult living as a gypsy. There were many times when we were not clean enough or warm enough or full enough or hydrated enough. Being dirty, cold, hungry and thirsty is honestly a miserable way to live. Somehow we managed to keep it together and stay focused on our goal of getting back to our home in Loeng Nok Tha. I wondered if Duey missed me, or Tunne and Farra. Life goes on, even after a good friend moves away.

The harsh way of the jungle was very different than our lives had been in the city. My family was subjected to the elements of hot, hot sun; to cool nights and heavy rains during monsoon season. During those times we stayed in caves on the higher grounds. This undesirable environment was a recipe for sickness, especially after bucketfuls of rain swept away the earth. The rains often stirred up a variety of strange insects with insatiable appetites. The jungle mosquitoes of

Thailand were one of the species of insects I was taught to be fearful of and to avoid at all costs, just as much as poisonous spiders and reptiles.

A specific parasite carried by the jungle mosquitoes in Southeast Asia were known to be the cause of a deadly disease called Malaria. Malaria is transmitted when the nasty mosquito pokes through the skin and draws blood. The parasite travels through the insect's saliva to the human bloodstream, where it then attacks the liver and multiplies. After about two weeks of spreading through the blood supply, the parasites then rip through the red blood cells, causing them to break down. When this happens, the symptoms begin taking effect. A high fever, headaches, anemia, heavy vomiting, shivering, joint and muscle pains are the first signs. Nine out of ten times death is the prognosis. Needless to say, it was a disease that no one wanted to experience.

I felt the mosquito bite me right in the back of the neck. My mother and I were picking mushrooms in the forest. The tender mushrooms were plentiful after the rains. Big, beautiful mushrooms were worth good money. I slapped the annoying insect and killed it. Then I just continued picking mushrooms because I didn't feel anything different.

At least, not right away.

Chapter

5

BY THE END OF THE WEEK I FELT A LITTLE 'not myself'. That's when I began seeing spots and getting hot flashes, but at the same time I felt so cold that my body shivered. My mother knew it was malaria when she felt my forehead. She tried brewing herbs in a stew from the forest and she boiled water to put steam near my skin for cleansing. But I just kept getting sicker and sicker. Every day I felt worse and eventually blacked out altogether.

The neighbors from a farm a few miles away came to fetch me with their donkey and cart. The back of the cart was filled with straw and a couple of blankets that my mother wrapped me in as she rode in the back of the wagon with me. The closest city was hours away in Si Saket. My mother prayed to the Buddha the whole way and held my hand in comfort, as I faded in and out of consciousness.

The ride seemed long but once we reached Si Saket, the farmer dropped us off at a hospital and then left. He couldn't have known as he made the journey home that we were unable to get admitted. At that time in Thailand, a hospital could refuse to treat patients if the patients did not have the means to pay for the healthcare. My mother did not have enough money to get us in, so despite my declining health, the hospital sent us away.

Desperate, my mother hailed a taxi cab next to the hospital entrance. A driver named Ellon stopped and we climbed in.

"My daughter is dying," she pleaded. "She is very sick but the hospital will not take us. Please help me."

Ellon drove us to the next hospital. He could see that I was very sick and was very sympathetic. Ellon agreed to take us at no charge. However, once again we were rejected from admittance to the next hospital. In fact, Ellon drove to every health clinic he could think of and the answer was the same each time. *"No money, no healthcare."* Even though a child's life was at stake, there was not one facility within Si Saket who would bend the rules.

So Ellon took matters upon himself to help us. I believe he was my Guardian Angel that day, if you believe in that sort of thing. There had to be a divine power that protected me. Maybe he just had a soft heart, or maybe he just liked my mother. Maybe he even had a family of his own, who knows. All I know is that I am thankful for his eagerness to save me.

He dropped us off in a safe place. "Stay here," Ellon instructed my mother. "I will be back for you and your daughter in three hours."

True to his word, the cab driver came back and with

enough cash to admit me into the hospital. It turns out the literal meaning of Ellon's name was the 'prince of angels'. How fitting, indeed.

That was where I was to be for the next three months. From the forest to the hospital, I was so severely sick that my mother feared for my life. The nurses told her it was one of the worst cases of malaria in children they had ever seen and that she had waited too long to get the proper treatment. In those days, the treatment required doses upon doses of varying medicines used to ease the fever, many of which had to be administered through an IV because I was in and out of consciousness to the point of delirium.

The fever escalated with no signs of letting up. Sometimes my body suffered such great convulsions that the nurses had to tie my arms and legs to the bed with white linens. I lost feeling in my legs and the circulation in my other extremities was very poor. I could not keep food down and was burning up, yet felt so chilly. Even the warm blankets they wrapped me in were not enough to keep me from feeling cold. Every time I tried to open my eyes – even just a sliver – it was very difficult.

My mother stayed close by my side the whole time; nursing me, caring for me and watching over me. She was such a good woman who kept me safe and alive. I wanted to repay her one day and reward her with a big fancy house of her own; one that she would never have to clean or work for ever again because I would hire maids and butlers for her. She had worked so hard and lived a very difficult life. My Mom was like a rose among thorns. Losing her daughter surely would have pushed her over the edge of depression, yet my mom hung on to hope with fierce resilience. She maintained a positive frame of mind, despite the great obstacles that lie across her path.

I was determined to live and see my dreams come to fruition, in part so that my mother could one day live the better life that she deserved, plus one that *I deserved* as well. Deep down, I knew that it was not my time to die yet, so I prayed and prayed and dreamed and dreamed.

Amazingly, I did start to recover after three months of near death illness. My fever dissipated and the severe headaches became minor disturbances. I was able to keep food down and began feeling better and better. And yes, I was thankful to be alive.

However, there was one major issue that greatly inhibited my feeling of joy for recovering a near death experience. My legs felt strange, like a couple of popsicle sticks that were stuck to my hips. Sadly, I realized I could not walk.

It was a bit like modern day physical therapy learning how to walk again. When you're a baby, you can't remember the process of learning to walk so it makes falling down less painful. Since you can't remember doing it, all of those lumps and bumps from toddlerhood just fade into the memory bank. Or perhaps kids are secretly made of rubber.

However, when you're a teenager and learning how to walk again, your brain plays tricks on you. Since your mind already knows how to walk because you have done it before, it's difficult to tell your legs what you want them to do. The bruises hurt worse when you fall and you certainly can remember the pain of falling more vividly.

Part of my process in learning to walk again was done by taking baby steps and using a cane made of native bamboo. Eventually, I did get faster and faster at walking, until a full recovery was made. However, I do still experience some aches in my joints to this day because of the malaria. Or maybe those pains can be attributed to the aging process, depending on how it is perceived.

Eventually, my father sold our plot of land near Cambodia after we had earned enough money by using and selling many of the resources that were there. The harvest that spring had been plentiful and my parents, sister and I had sold every last seed, tomato and mushroom the land would bear. So finally, our family was able to go back to our home in Loeng Nok Tha.

The timing could not have been better, for things were getting hotter on all of the Thai borders at that time. In fact, Loeng Nok Tha was only 25 km from the Northeast border of Laos, making it an ideal spot for the military to construct a giant airstrip.

The project was called Operation Crown and it was to become the main airstrip for the Commonwealth allied forces leading into the Vietnam War. Built by the royal engineers of British and Australian sappers for the military, this airfield also became the runway where the US Air Force departed to bomb Laos and Vietnam. That fact remained hidden from the world for some time, but history has since brought it into the limelight, as past workers have come forward to speak the truth. Back then, the soldiers were told that the airstrip was going to be used primarily as a way to enhance the Thai economy, giving our government access to bring precious goods in and out of the country.

When the military came in to build this great airstrip, it really helped the local Thai economy. The airstrip brought many jobs to the people of Loeng Nok Tha, as well as more people buying and selling to stimulate the local businesses. My father had also helped to build this airstrip when he was working as a carpenter.

The arduous walk to Loeng Nok Tha was filled with much anxiety for me. As the days of gypsy living fell behind me in the shadows of desperation, I thought of the life I had left behind and the road ahead. With my bamboo cane gently leading the way, I thought of the temple and the small school I had not seen for a few years.

Losing my academic opportunities had put me behind where I wanted to be. The bout with malaria had been another setback, as well. As I made the journey back home with my family, I wondered if I would be dumber than when I left. Had I gone from being an honor roll student with big dreams of fame and fortune to just a mere peasant who was trying to survive in the world?

No, no, no. I was very smart. I debated with my inner conscious and reconfirmed my conviction for what were seemingly girlish dreams. You know the kind that seems unrealistic? I was still only a young girl with a bright future. Going home was to become my chance for self betterment. These were some of the thoughts that churned in my pensive mind.

Once we arrived back in the familiar community, my father repaid the loan sharks to buy our house back. Even though I had been raised there, it was definitely strange to be home again. We took down the boards and washed down the furniture. Everything was dusty and dingy with a gross smell. My room seemed smaller than I had remembered.

I thought things would go back to normal for us. At least, whatever you might consider to be normal. And it was, for awhile. My father got a job doing carpentry work. With the military in town, there were many more job opportunities than ever before. The Americans brought money and supported local businesses. The Loeng Nok Tha airstrip played a vital role prior to and leading into the Vietnam War.

At that time I was a young girl of about fourteen. Whenever I saw the soldiers in town, to me they seemed big and scary. Especially the black ones. Americans came in so many different sizes and colors. They all seemed very tall, with big muscles and much ethnic diversity. Their accents were expressive and many of them used their hands to talk to the Thai people because of the communication barrier. A few of them were very friendly. The soldiers sometimes whistled at the young girls who curiously hung out on the street, as if they were dogs.

As I neared the age of fifteen, I had a burning urge to fulfill my dreams. I longed to escape. I dreamed of being successful and wanted so badly to be on TV. I wanted to be a millionaire!

Sadly, my father had not learned his lesson when we lost our house and moved to the roughest terrain in Thailand. Even though none of us had enjoyed living as gypsies for the past three or four years, unfortunately his regression to the lure of alcohol could not be helped. He went back to his old ways. The allure of boozing and gambling was like a seductive playground for my father and he could not resist.

Therefore, our life at home was not ideal. My mother was distraught whenever my father left for a night or two, or sometimes more. She had worked so hard to get us back to where we were. She cried often and was very depressed. When he did come home, my father was drunk and apologetic. My parents often fought and it was not a happy situation for my sister and me.

Although I tried to remain positive, deep down I was depressed, too. We were all very disappointed in my father's lack of consideration for his family. He was the one who had put us in this predicament.

Quietly, I resented him. I loved Dad, but not with the same unbridled love I had for my mother. It was more of a love based on obligation, such as one is expected to love a member of their family even when that person doesn't treat them very well.

Once again, my father's regression put our family in a tough situation. He didn't show up for work some days to his carpentry job and on the days he did, he was either drunk or hung-over. I couldn't take it anymore.

By then I was only fifteen years old, just a budding flower that was about to bloom. I decided it was time to go and find my own way in the world. I simply could not live in that house with my father any longer. My quest for fame and fortune was not going to be hampered by my father's reputation.

I had no plan, not really. I was oblivious to the lurking dangers of the world outside what I knew. Yet I realized the need to determine if there really was something better 'out there'. My lifelong longing got the better of my curiosity and my home life became intolerable. These two factors became the festering desire to go. To just go. Were my dreams to come true one day or were they just a figment of my daydreams?

There was only one way to find out.

The fluffy white clouds and riches were out there and I knew they were destined to be mine one day. Soon, I hoped. For these reasons I made my decision.

Packed with nothing more than a small bag of big dreams and fearless regrets, I ran away.

Chapter

6

RUM-KACHUNK. RUM-KACHUNK. RUM-kachunk. Rum-kachunk ... the spirited sound of the train rolling over the tracks lulled me into a trance, as I dazed out of the cloudy window.

My mind raced even faster than the train, thinking of many things ahead, as well as those people whom I had left behind. Especially my mother.

She had stood teary eyed in the driveway as I left that morning. She had begged me not to go. She had worn her Sunday dress to see me off, a cream-colored cotton with bright hibiscus print that she had sewn herself.

"Please, Nuensie..." she sobbed, as the tears streamed down her cheeks. "You are too young. Please don't go!"

"But I must leave mother. You know why. I must find my way in life and I am ready to pursue my dreams," I assured her. "Don't worry, I will be back to get you one day. I promise. I will bring my riches and will whisk you away. I will build you a big house where you will be happy and live in peace with everything you need. I promise, Mama."

NUENSIE SUKU

I hugged Mama so tight and for so long I could still feel her embrace with me as I rode the train. Using money I had scrounged and saved for many months, I was able to buy a train ticket to Korat. The money was bundled up in a little wad about the size of a tennis ball, with a rubber band holding it together. Besides, I was used to being poor so having a little money of my own made me feel good. I knew that I could find things to eat for about the equivalent of a quarter per sitting. So in theory, my small wad should have been enough to last me a few weeks.

The only plan was to take a train somewhere, although I did not know exactly where it would lead me or what I would do once I arrived in Korat. Sheer courage and prepubescent hopefulness was my inspiration. Like a hobo, I hopped on the train and sat down in one of the cold seats.

Even though it was my first time on a train, I think I enjoyed the ride simply for the relief I felt in leaving my hometown, a place filled with bad memories and stagnant opportunities. The other passengers had their heads down or stared out the window. Everyone was deep within their own lives and problems.

After I got off the train, I didn't really know what to do next. For a few hours I sat on a bench at the train station in Korat. Another passenger had tapped me once the train stopped. "We're here," said a friendly old Thai man. His face was filled with wrinkles around his eyebrows and mouth; perhaps from either laughing or scowling too much the creases had made their mark on his face permanently.

"Thank you," I smiled. "I guess I must have been daydreaming and forgotten to get off."

The truth is I had no place to be. I didn't know where I was going or what I would do when I got there. Wherever 'there' was.

After sitting and observing people at the train station for what seemed like many hours, I noticed a number of interracial couples. There were a lot of men from America and Britain. Some were holding hands or walking with women from Thailand. It was my first real encountering with American men. They looked just as big and scary as ever, dressed in military apparel of green and blue. They seemed confident and forceful in demeanor. Some were smiling and others were stoic. They had nice teeth and short, short hair styles. I had seen them in my hometown before, working on the airstrip as the war with Vietnam got underway with full vengeance.

Growing up, my fellow students and I had never really known that much about Eastern countries. We had been fearful of foreigners, although most people whom we had encountered were kind and some of the soldiers had even brought us food. It was not until the mid-sixties that we began seeing more of the soldiers coming to Thailand. It turns out there was a prominent Air Force Base in Korat.

One of the couples at the train station even had a baby with them. The young Thai woman carried the baby in a sling across her chest, as she walked alongside the man in a green military suit. Their baby had light skin like his father, yet with the distinctive Asian eyes of his mother. The baby's hair was fluffy and dark brown. I couldn't help but to think how beautiful their child was with his internationally blended features.

The Thailand woman was dressed nice, too. It caught my attention. While sitting on the bench at the train station that day, I came to the realization that perhaps by marrying an American man one day, I could finally be afforded the lifestyle I so longed for.

"What are you doing here by yourself, young miss?" said a woman's voice. Startled, I blinked and looked up to find a woman in a blue sleeveless blouse and velvet skirt standing over me. "It's not safe here for a young girl, especially one as pretty as you are," she went on. "Someone will do you harm here."

"Well, I really don't have any place to go," I replied.

"Where are your parents? Are you an orphan?" she further probed.

"They are back in Loeng Nok Tha. I ran away," was my shortened answer.

She thought for a moment and fidgeted with her satchel. "Come with me," she said. "You can stay at my house and you will be safe there. If you stay here, you may get raped or murdered. This is no place for a young girl to be. How old are you?"

"Fifteen," I answered.

"Come," she beckoned, with a tender smile. "I will take you to my home. You can do some housekeeping for me in exchange for a place to stay. Alright?"

"Certainly," I replied graciously. I didn't have any other options so it sounded good, even though she was a complete stranger.

Although neither she nor I realized it at the time, her sincere attempt to keep me out of the path of danger led me straight into the Lion's Den.

Her name was Hansa and she was a woman in her early thirties by my best guess. Hansa dressed nicely and was well-spoken (even somewhat sophisticated) by Thai standards. It was evident that she was educated. She nodded and said "Hello" in English to a few of the Americans as we walked together through the train station, as well as "Sawatdee" to a few of the Thai people; which means both Hello and Goodbye in Thai.

Her house was off the beaten path, just on the outskirts of Karat. It was a humble home, yet tastefully decorated. The smell of a cigar filled the room when we entered.

"Wait here," Hansa instructed as we entered. "I must tell my husband that you are here."

Hansa left me alone for a few minutes and I looked around. In the hallway there were pictures hung of Hansa with an American soldier. Her husband was in Thailand from the US, stationed at the Royal Thai Air Force Base (RTAFB) in Korat. During the war with Vietnam it was the biggest frontline facility used by the US military. Although many of the commanders were Thai officers, Hansa's husband happened to be stationed at Camp Friendship. This was one of the Southern posts adjacent to the Korat Air Base.

Her marriage to the American military man explained Hansa's well educated demeanor. As the wife of one of the US officers who was assigned to the tactical fighting operation near Korat, Hansa was able to live the very best lifestyle imaginable for a woman of Thai decent. It was evident that her husband took great care of her. She had fine china, beautiful woven rugs and colorful pillows artfully decorated throughout her home.

Hansa's husband provided everything, from the Americanized housing to the food and possessions. *'Is this the ticket to wealth?'* I wondered under my breath. *'Do I have to marry a rich American soldier to finally live the life I have always dreamed?'*

One noticeable thing that I found most intriguing was Hansa's superb collection of books. She had a whole bookcase filled with poetry, fiction, non-fiction and autobiographies. As I thumbed through a few of them I noticed they were mostly printed in English.

When I was a youngster in school, we were so poor that we had used small chalkboards and erasers only. Of course, I had seen books before but not very often. Only the affluent people owned books.

"Come in and let me see you!" roared a gruff voice. It was Hansa's husband hollering at me from the kitchen. When I walked in, I saw the man who appeared in the pictures that Hansa had hanging in the hallway.

"Nuensie, meet my husband." Hansa was stood next to him, proudly. "He said it was fine if you want to stay with us. I will show you to your room down the hall."

"How old are you, young lady?" he asked with a raised eyebrow, as he puffed on his cigar.

"Seventeen Sir," I lied.

"Where's your pa and ma?" he asked.

"Well they're home in Loeng Nok Tha," I answered.

"I see," he said, studying me. "Show her to her room darling." He patted Hansa on the rump as she walked towards me.

She took me down a hallway to the back of their home. While walking past the bathroom, I noticed another room with a door ajar. There was a man in there, but I didn't get a good look at him because his back was turned and he was sleeping. The light of the door crack shone on the side of his face, but not enough to disturb him or make his face available for a glimpse.

"That's one of my husband's new recruits," whispered Hansa, before I could ask. My eyes probed her inquisitively so she offered an explanation. "They haven't placed him in his own housing yet, so he's staying with us for a couple of weeks."

I nodded.

"Your room is this one," Hansa pointed to the door across the hall.

It was pleasant, yet plain. There was just a bed, dresser and white quilt. Only a mirror and a framed picture hung on the walls.

"I'll let you get settled in. Then you can come back to the kitchen and I will fix us a meal," said Hansa.

I felt somewhat comfortable as I dined with them. As comfortable as you can be in a stranger's home. I was very grateful for the place to stay and a roof over my head. If I had not met Hansa, I would have perhaps been still sitting on that bench at the train station, wondering where to go or what to do. It was nice of her to have taken me in.

For a few days, everything was fine. Hansa's husband and the man who stayed with them were gone on a mission but were due to return later in the week. I cleaned and cooked for her and we talked some. I even opened up to her a little bit about my dreams of becoming rich.

Hansa then confided in me, too. She shared with me the possibility of marrying an American one day so that I could live the lifestyle that I so dreamed of. In her eyes, the shortest and most direct route to being taken care of was to become a 'kept' woman. She didn't seem to mind and was perfectly content with her arrangement. In fact, I believed that Hansa loved her husband and did not just marry him for the lifestyle he could provide.

THE QUEST FOR SERENDIPITY

The men returned a few days later. I finally got a good look at Hansa's husband's co-worker. He stared me down with creepy eyes as we all sat at dinner. I felt downright uncomfortable for the first time all week. He had a gruffness about him that was too strange to put my finger on. It was not his appearance, it was his demeanor. I couldn't understand the things he said because I didn't speak English. However I knew he made comments about me by the way he looked at me and then spoke to Hansa's husband with a loud chuckle. You can just tell when someone's talking about you, even if you don't understand their language. His gestures and body language were the qualities that gave away his intent. Eventually I excused myself and went to my room.

Later that evening, I heard the men downstairs playing cards. They were loud and I couldn't understand what they said. They drank, laughed, smoked cigarettes, growled and were just plain loud.

I tried to ignore them and rest my eyes in an attempt to fall asleep. As I lay there, I couldn't help but think that this was exactly the type of life I had wanted to get away from. My father's booze fests and card games were very similar.

Maybe I dozed off, because the next thing I remember was feeling a cold steel knife at the base of my throat. I froze.

Instant terror filled my mind, as the silhouette of the man across the hall became familiar. It took a minute for my eyes to adjust in the darkness. His hot breath smelled of booze and cigarettes, which matched the foulness of his presence.

"Don't you make a move. Or I'll slit your throat."

My eyes grew as big as saucers as my mind pumped with fear and adrenaline, as if someone had punctured my heart with a fierce needle. Even though I didn't understand what he said, I certainly understood the knife on my throat and what was about to happen.

He lowered his knife and I grabbed the sheets for dear life as he ripped a cruel tear through my nightgown. "NO! Please no…" I cried as the tears streamed down my cheeks, though no one could see them in the darkness of the quiet room. Nobody heard my cries, my screams … or were they just a whisper?

As the big burly man unzipped his pants, he looked at me with a smirk of disgust. With the knife still tightly squeezed amidst the palm of his hand, he grabbed me by the hair and positioned himself over my face.

I had never seen a man's penis. He stuck the strange and smelly thing right in my face. After drinking and smoking cigarettes all night he had a sour fume that matched his evil personality. "Get to work, Princess." He ordered.

My lips were clamped shut, so he shoved the knife up against my mouth. "I swear if you don't get to work I'm gonna cut your pretty little face into a hundred pieces."

All I could do was obey. I opened my mouth as he rammed his engorged tool in and out of my throat. He was gagging me and choking me until I thought I would suffocate or throw up from fear and the act itself.

After his thing got even bigger he pushed me down on the

bed and covered my mouth with his dirty hand. He set the knife carefully on the floor next to the bed and said, "Don't get any ideas or you will die."

Still covering my mouth, he pushed my torn nightgown off until I was nearly naked. I lay there in terror, not daring to move. I thought about grabbing the knife down beside the bed but he still had a stronghold on my mouth as he pinned my head down.

"Spread your legs," he ordered. I clamped them together, trying to yell through his sweaty hand. "Shut the hell up!"

"NOOOOO! Please...." I tried to shout through his palm but all it sounded like was a murmur of desperation.

He savagely ripped my underwear and pushed my legs open. I thought he would break me in half. Still trying to save myself from the horror of what he was about to do, I scrambled to push him off and yelled underneath his grasp. That only pissed him off even more.

Angrily he shouted, "Stop moving, you little bitch! Be still! You can make this easy or you can make it difficult. It's up to you."

With that, he wrangled my hands behind my back so I could no longer push him. He was much stronger than I was. It was like a fawn trying to fight off a grizzly bear.

Taking what he did not deserve to have, he shoved himself inside of me as I cried in pain. It felt like someone shoved a baseball bat inside of me and I could barely breathe as he slammed his burly physique into my body. The pain was excruciating. He got so zealous that he rammed my tiny frame up against the headboard and I thought he was going to knock me unconscious or kill me. When his hand got away from my mouth for a moment, I let out a scream so he stuffed a pillow over my face, nearly suffocating me.

I couldn't see anymore, all I could do was feel the sharp pain and ripping of my body as he suffocated and raped me. I was so terrified I just wished that I was dead so the pain would stop and it would all be over.

Regrettably, that was only the beginning of a night that was to become the most grisly experience of my life. It made all of the material things I had ever lacked pale in comparison to value. I would have given everything right then to prevent that from happening.

That night, I was raped repeatedly. He tore my insides as he had his way with me, forcing me to comply with all of his demands. I felt like a ragdoll that was tossed around against the stiff wood of the wall and headboard. My ears, hands and nose were smashed into the pillow as he flipped me over. I could barely breathe.

As morning approached I felt bruised, dehydrated and like I truly wanted to die. The foul aroma of booze and cigarettes haunted me for many months thereafter. Of course, I wished I had made better plans than running away to Korat. I thought of my mother's plea to make me stay in Loeng Nok Tha and of Hansa's words of wisdom; "You can't stay here. Someone will do you harm."

I wondered if Hansa knew. Had she led me to her home with the intent of knowing that her husband's friend would rape me? Maybe it had all been a setup. At that moment I hated her, too. I hated them all.

I drifted off throughout the night, in a state of exhaustion and hopelessness. Each time I woke, he was still there, on top of me... smothering me... bruising me. Shame and horror washed over me in waves of regret, like the fearless typhoon that tears down everything in its path. I was destroyed inside and out.

The ordeal lasted too long; well into the next day. I could barely walk, but when the drunken American finally passed out, I slipped out from underneath his brutal grasp and slithered through the crack.

Blood was everywhere and my soiled clothes had been ruined because they were on the floor near the bed. The only thing I had time to grab was a thin blouse and halter skirt to cover up with. I crawled silently to the door and carefully peered into the hall.

Had this been a setup? Had Hansa offered me the place to stay, knowing that her husband's friend was a brutal rapist?

No, it could not be.

Hansa was in the kitchen as I crept slowly down the hall with my back brushing gently against the wall. When she saw me, she shook her head from side to side. "Nuensie, Nuensie," she called to me with arms outstretched.

"How could you let this happen to me?" I sobbed. "I trusted you. I confided in you. "Why? WHY!"

"I'm so sorry," she implored. "I swear, Nuensie. I didn't know this was going to happen. Don't worry, you won't get pregnant."

"Why didn't you come? Why didn't you help me if you knew he was in there?" I begged for an answer.

"I ..." she stammered, not sure what to say.

Hansa's reassuring words were nothing more than meaningless gestures of short lived friendships.

"Please, Nuensie. Take this and go!" she gathered a papaya, two tomatoes, a sweater and a few coins. "You'll need something to eat. Go back home, to your parents. I tried to keep you safe but alas, I have invited you into the darkest fire of hell. I am very sorry. You must go, before he wakes up."

So I fled. When I left Hansa's home, I did not look back, not even once. Leaving a trail of blood, I ran as fast as I could. My body was badly bruised all over and still bleeding. My leg muscles were like jello. I just wanted to feel clean and get the foul smell off me. The blood with its iron odor and the cigarette and sweat smells. Everything. My soul felt like it was ripped out of my chest, as if I was watching myself from above the clouds.

Despite the crippling pain, I ran and ran as fast as I could, through the rain. The skies opened up as the monsoon rains began, with giant drops raining hard in a painful shower of pellets. The buckets of water coming down from the skies made the blood streak through my clothing, which now stuck to my skin with dripping transparency. Shivering, I just kept running, thinking, crying, and repeating the horrifying incident over and over again in my mind.

Perhaps the most tragic part of the night was that even though I had lived a life of poverty, I still always had one thing that could never be taken away. My innocence. And now – more than ever before – I truly had nothing left in the world.

It was at that moment when I came to the realization that running and running for no reason was futile, because there was no way to escape from myself. I slowed to a walk and welcomed the rain's cleansing wash as I looked up and prayed. Finally, I could run nor walk no more.

Chapter

7

EVERY LITTLE GIRL DREAMS OF HER wedding day. No matter what country she is from or what traditions are followed within her country of upbringing, in every girl's dreams she is blissfully happy. She imagines being led to her Prince Charming by her proud father, who gives her away to her husband-to-be. Depending on the country and the customs therewith, those wedding dreams may vary from one little girl to the next. However, the theme is much the same.

Meet Prince Charming.

Fall in love.

Prince Charming gets down on bended knee and asks for her hand in marriage, customarily with a beautiful diamond or precious gemstone.

She says yes.

A wedding is planned.

The father walks his daughter, the bride, down the aisle to her future husband.

They tie the knot.

THE QUEST FOR SERENDIPITY

The groom carries his bride over the threshold and they make mad passionate love all night, as she finally gives herself to the man she has saved for that "forever" love.

As I learned the hard way, when that fantasy gets yanked away by a rapist, so does the dream. The virgin's dream is forever discarded, along with the self respect and the normal confidence of a teen girl. Her innocence is shattered, along with the possibility of purity. She feels ruined.

It was cold as the rain fell, almost melting as it touched my skin. Finally in the middle of the woods, I huddled into a ball near a fallen tree. The moss was my pillow and I drifted away, wondering what it would be like to meet the Great Buddha.

Gradual exhaustion and fatigue overtook me. I felt like I had been pounded into the ground like a well digger that looks for water, with its powerful steel hammer and loud rapping that pulsated through my core.

I felt a shadow above my head as my eyes tried to adjust to see the face of a man standing over me. For a moment I became fearful, as I tried to make out the man's figure through crusty tears and dried up blood and mud. Dressed in an American soldier's attire, for just a sliver of a second I feared it might be him ... the monster who had stolen that sacred part of me, my very soul.

It was not.

The man sat down next to me and gently stroked my chin and cheek. "Who did this to you?" he asked angrily. But I did not understand him.

He took his coat off and wrapped it around me. I melted from exhaustion, hoping the man would not do me any harm, as I was too helpless to fight for my body or my life. Then he scooped me up and carried me to a military hospital at the air force base in Korat. While there he learned what happened to me.

"She has been raped and badly beaten," explained a doctor. "Do you know her?"

"No," said the man. "I came across her on my way to pick up a new recruit."

"She needs stitches and lots of rest. Someone really beat this poor little girl up," the doctor said.

For two days I rested at the hospital as the nurses fixed me up and gave me a morphine drip, along with some food and water. The whole time, the American man never left my side. He sat in a chair next to the bed, watching me as I drifted in and out of consciousness.

Just like a guardian angel, his name was Peter and he watched over me and protected me. Pete was the nickname he used. He was a decorated officer and highly respected leader in the Air Force.

Since I couldn't speak English, I was unable to explain to him what happened. But I trusted him, at least a little bit. After I was released from the hospital, Pete took me back to his house. Only the higher ranking officers had their own housing apart from the soldiers. His was a clean two bedroom within the Air Force base complex.

THE QUEST FOR SERENDIPITY

It was to become my home for the next eight months, where Pete allowed me to stay with him. In all that time, he never touched me inappropriately or tried to take advantage of me. He was always a gentleman. The language barrier made our relationship one of little talking, yet we developed a unique understanding of each other in the duration of our cohabitation.

From everything I observed, Pete was a hard working man. Every day he went to work and came home to a clean home. I did all of his housekeeping, although he was a very clean guy by nature. He provided food, shelter, clothing and everything I needed.

Sometimes he would talk to me, although I never fully understood what he said. We learned a few words of each other's language but our communication was one of pointing, smiling and hand signals. Silent talk. Pete was a musician and loved to play his guitar. Every night he sang and played to me. His music was a serenade to my soul as I began to heal from my terrible ordeal.

During the first few days of living with him, I was so afraid that I locked my door every night. Although Pete never implied any harm or ill will towards me, nor had he ever taken advantage of me or touched me, after the rape I was on high alert and unease. I often had nightmares but instead of a face there was a monster on top of me. It was green, muscular and ugly.

It was Pete's beautiful music that helped me to heal. As he

sang, I remembered the contests I had won at the State Fair as a child, as well as my mother's encouragement to win. I missed her dearly.

Although my dreams had been scarred, they were still wishes for one day in my future. I still longed to become wealthy, famous and maybe even to become a celebrity!

Pete not only housed me during the time I lived with him, he bought me clothes, shoes and even jewelry. He asked for nothing in return. One special necklace Pete gave me was one I kept for most of my adulthood. It was a special peace symbol. Amid the center was a small ruby, which signified great devotion of the heart. In the late sixties, the peace symbol was very popular among war protestors but those distinctive three branches have remained popular to this very day.

These tokens became treasures of the friendship between Pete and me. It was almost as if he was saying; "*Get the peace back*".

I never really learned the personal background about Pete because we were unable to communicate to one another. My hunch was that he was a married man who treated women with respect, unlike the American soldier who had raped me. Perhaps he just enjoyed my company and having someone there. He was a good-looking guy of about 25 or 30. Pete stood at about 5' 11" and looked much the part of a dignified, clean cut military officer. He was educated, classy and very kind. Much like the angel, Saint Peter. He didn't drink or smoke and rarely associated with his subordinates, except while at work.

Occasionally we went into the town together to buy food. People respected Pete and some saluted him when we were out in public. It was strange having a friend you couldn't talk to, but somehow I just enjoyed his presence and the feeling of security he gave me.

After living with him for about eight months, he pointed to a chair as his non-verbal way of asking me to sit. He tried talking to me, asking if I had a family that I wanted to return home to? However, I could not understand the questions he asked. English sounded like gibberish and even his Pictionary-like gestures could not be interpreted by my lack of the English dialect.

He smiled and gave up, patting me on the shoulder. "It's okay, little one." Then the next day he brought his friend's girlfriend over who spoke Thai. It was the first time we were really able to speak to each other by way of an interpreter.

The interpreter explained to me that Pete had been ordered to return to the U.S. He wanted to know if I would like to return to my family, or did I even have a family to go home to? He didn't want to leave me stranded so he was trying to figure out what to do with me. It was nice that he cared about my well-being even though he had to leave. Pete was a protector.

I nodded yes, even though I did not plan on returning home for good. Pete explained through the interpreter that he would give me enough money to remain at his house for a few more months, even after he left. He had to leave within a few days. Pete had been trying to say goodbye and explain all of this to me the day before, although I could not understand him.

For the next few days, he continued serenading me with his guitar and we enjoyed each other's company. I helped him prepare to leave, doing his laundry and folding his clothes while he was gone during the day. Nobody had ever cared for me like Pete had. Especially not a man – except maybe Duey – but even he had been a childhood friend more than a real male companion. Pete's kindness and compassion, as well as his beautiful guitar playing and singing were like warm rays of sunshine after a fierce storm.

The $25 a day allowance Pete left me was more than generous to finish my stay there. In fact, most of it I saved with the intent to bring home to my mother and to help my family. Pete hugged me when he left and said a few kind words that I did not understand. I knew that he was special and his genuine smile said it all.

After Pete left, it was very quiet and lonely. I grew saddened by his absence as I tried to figure out what I should do with myself next. A chapter of my life was nearing a close, yet I was anxious to keep reading. What would unfold for me was unforeseen, like the anticipation of a new adventure for a brave explorer.

Chapter

8

"**H**ELLO MAMA," I SAID, STARTLING HER one day as she was winding down after a long afternoon of picking fruit.

Shocked, she squealed with delight at the sight of me coming through the door. My mother jumped out of her seat and squealed, "My Nuensie! My Nuensie!" She wrapped her arms around me in a warm embrace that seemed to last forever.

Upon leaving Korat that very morning on the train back to Loeng Nok Tha, I had wondered how she would react to my return home. She was excited, to say the very least. So was my little sister.

"I have missed you so much," she said as the tears rolled down her cheeks.

"Open your hand," I said with a smile.

She looked at me inquisitively as I laid a ball of money in her hand that I had saved from Pete's generosity. "Oh my goodness, Nuensie! Thank you!" she said, overjoyed.

"That's not all, Mamaa." I reached into my satchel and

pulled out a few jewelry pieces that Pete had given me, as well.

"Where did you get this? What have you been doing all year?" she hugged me again. "I have missed, you, oh daughter of mine!"

Even my father was happy to see me. We all shared a meal with some food I had brought with me from town. I was careful with my money the whole time I was away and was proud to offer all of it to my family. They were equally as pleased with my efforts.

"I'm not staying," I blurted out at dinner. "I'm just making a pit stop here and then I must move on. I am destined to be famous, remember?"

My mother replied, "Nuensie, you're going to become somebody. I just know it. Ever since you were a little girl you've had a special gift for entertaining. Don't let anyone hold you back from those goals."

"Mom, one day I'm going to marry a rich American man and come back to build you a big house!" I said proudly, as if it had already been accomplished.

We enjoyed some quality time together for the next few days. I didn't tell my mother about the rape. Some things are just better left unsaid, like quiet mysteries that become secrets we never share. After four or five days together, I set off once again for another journey to an undetermined place. Intuition was to be my inner guide and mentor.

"Always be honest with what you do," my Mom said as

she looked into my eyes. "I mean it. Never steal for money and always work hard."

I nodded. "Okay, Mama."

"Be honest first and foremost and the Buddha will reward you with the life you deserve," she added.

When I left home for the second time, I made the journey to Udon on the northeast region of Thailand. The railway went straight into the capital and at that time it was a booming town, partly because of the erection and placement of the Udon Royal Thai Air Force Base. During the Vietnam War, there were many U.S. soldiers stationed there as a vital base for combat and air traffic into and out of Vietnam and Laos.

Because of its position within Thailand, Udon was bustling with foreigners and native Thai people who became educated and wealthier due to the economic boost in the community. This enabled many Thai people to gain recognition by the outside world, even some who had remained far behind the curtains of anonymity for entire lifetimes. Hence, many of the Udon citizens created new goods or products that could be marketed to the outside world.

I had heard through gossip and through the news that there were many Americans in Udon now, which made the city an appealing choice for me to visit. My gut told me to go there. By then I had just turned sixteen and felt freed and worldly, like a woman coming into my own.

When I first arrived in Udon, I didn't really know what

to do with myself. I went to a bar to try to find a job. There were plenty of pretty women around town to ask where the hotspots were.

"Any bar will take a pretty young girl," winked one of the Thai girls who stood outside of the marketplace. She was dressed nice, if not somewhat provocative. "You'll have no problem getting a job here and the American men will eat you right up." At first I didn't know what she meant, but soon discovered the lifestyle of the Thai women who worked in Udon.

I found a job at a go-go bar, which is a loose term referring to the go-go dancers who worked at the local nightclubs in Thailand. Probably since the sixties, go-go bars have come to represent a different connotation; one for open-minded patrons who used those types of establishments as a place to meet women. Even still, the performers are often lured by money to do more than just dance for the sex-starved men who go there. This was particularly true during the Vietnam War, when the ratio of lonely men far outweighed the women. The soldiers were far, far away from their girlfriends and wives. And many more didn't even have any women back home to worry about.

Depending on the level of police meddling, the go-go bars offered explicit entertainment. In fact, some of the nightclubs were nicknamed 'ping pong shows', for obvious implications. Some of the dancers even bared it all by the end of their dance routines. Most were young Thai women trying to make their way in the world using any means necessary.

Of course, when I was hired at a go-go bar called the "*Tha Phrachan*" (which literally means "Moon Pier") I did not classify or perceive myself to be one of those girls who could be tempted to the afterhours type of entertaining. Subjecting to the life of an escort or call girl was never in the plans. Then again, I suppose no girl ever truly plans to become a call girl. It just happens when you open yourself up to that type of lifestyle.

Normally I just sat with men and had a drink. Nearly all of them were lonely soldiers. I kept them company and flirted with them. I made them feel good about themselves, even though deep down I did not feel good about myself. No sex took place with any of the customers at first, but when I began having trouble paying my rent and saw how easy and how much money some of the more experienced girls took home every night, my feelings about the profession began to change, mainly for survival's sake.

There was pressure from the bar owner, too. He was not native Thai, although he did have Thailand in his blood. The owner was actually a British lad who came to Thailand about a decade prior, just to find a long lost relative.

Regardless of how he got there, the bar owner was a ruthless character. He treated the women who worked for him pretty well, but there was definitely a lot of pressure to do more. Nothing was ever good enough for him. When he was angry, he called everything and everyone 'bloody'. I never understood why until many years later that the English use bloody as a swear word.

Between the pressure from the club owner and the peer pressure from many of the other girls – as well as not having the money I desperately needed – it was inevitable that I was destined to become a call girl in Udon.

Throughout my adulthood, the secret life I led as an escort was a shame I held internally. Looking back, I realize there was no shame for me or for many of the other girls who were just caught in that circle of survival. When you have nothing and the only thing you have to depend on is yourself to make it in the world, 'your own self' will do whatever is needed to survive.

There was part of me that also had not recovered from the rape. I still felt shameful and remorseful for getting in that predicament to begin with. My self esteem had drifted down the river and emptied into a giant sea, just waiting for some hero to come along and throw me a life preserver so I could get out of the mode of drowning in lost regrets and what-ifs.

Since I was unable to save myself for marriage, I justified my behavior with the philosophy that if I was going to have sex anyway then I might as well make money. Surprisingly, it was one of the best paying gigs a young girl could land. It's unfortunate that the lost innocence of a young woman can lead her down a path of immoral concepts.

I suppose I could have done something else with my life

while in Udon, yet somehow I was meant to go there. Little did I know that the answer would soon reveal itself to me.

But the real reason I chose to work at the go-go bar instead of becoming a housekeeper, sales clerk, waitress or something ordinary was not motivated solely by money. I most enjoyed the opportunity to be up on the stage every night, singing. *Tha Phrachan* customers loved my singing and many of the regulars came in at least a few nights every week just to watch me sing. It was the little girl inside of me that had always dreamed of singing and dancing, therefore even despite the crude circumstances of a nightclub environment, it was finally my chance to shine and soak up the spotlight.

When I sang, I loved the attention. I loved it as much as I loved singing itself. I loved the whistling, clapping and crowd of men hooting and hollering. Like a pack of hungry wolves, they howled at every performance.

"That's quite a pretty voice you have, just like a songbird of the South," said a man's voice as I finished my singing performance one evening.

Of course, I didn't really understand his language so I thought he was just another customer coming on to me. "As they say, flattery will get you everywhere," I replied flirtatiously in Thai.

He beckoned to an interpreter. "I'm Gus."

I introduced myself to him as Nancy, which I often used whenever meeting the Americans. It sounded as close to Nuensie as you can get out of a Thai translation.

Gus and I had great chemistry. He had an interesting accent compared to many of the other soldiers. It was because he was raised within one of the Southern states within the U.S., which gave him a distinctive drawl.

"Yer just the prettiest thing I've seen since I've been in this Godforsaken place," said Gus. I thought he seemed adorable, yet manly. However, he was not so unlike many of the other American soldiers I had met and gone out with.

Something about Gus made my heart flutter a bit more than most men. It was his confidence. He took a strong liking to me and we went out a few times for drinks, which usually ended with a nightcap at his place. Gus was a passionate guy.

After seeing him frequently for about a week, one day Gus said; "If you're gonna date me I don't want you to be a call girl anymore. You're going to be my girl now, okay?"

He then put me up in an apartment and offered to take care of me financially and otherwise. Gus paid me enough every month to help me afford to send money to my mother and sister, as well. I was happy with the arrangement because I no longer had to sleep with different men just to come up with enough money to live, eat and pay my rent. For me, it was an ideal situation even though at times I felt that Gus was quite controlling in his behaviors. Our sole reason for hooking up was so that I would no longer have to exploit myself and sell my body in exchange for living, because in essence that was what I had to do just to survive.

In Gus's mind, I was '*his girl*' and that was that. Since he took care of me and paid my way, his philosophy was that he could pretty much do whatever he wanted, while I was not allowed to follow suit. Hence, Gus stepped out on me quite often. He slept with other women throughout the time that we were dating. Although it bothered me, I continued to stay with him because it was still better than my situation had been working as a call girl. So I allowed it to happen.

Sometimes I turned the other way, but other times my fury got the better of me. My father had also stepped out on my mother many times throughout their marriage. It seemed to be the "accepted norm" for women in Thailand to tolerate this type of behavior. In fact, many of Thai men of that generation had multiple wives! Over time, that attitude has changed as Thai women have become more independent. Today it would be grounds for a breakup to discover that your man has been unfaithful.

Back then, it was not. It was bothersome, yet more accepted. I did as I was told and played the perfect role of Gus's girl, staying faithfully by his side through thick and thin despite his lack of regard for monogamy.

Thinking back, I feel like I have always been abused by men in one way or another. From my father's gambling and drinking addictions that caused our lifelong financial disparity, to the rape and even the men I was to meet thereafter, I had never been truly respected as a woman until much later in life.

In my mind part of that is attributed to wealth. Men treat

affluent women differently, especially those who have their own business and who are successful. Women who are weak or dependent become a walking target for the wrong type of man because they are more apt to accept the abusive behavior, not realizing their own self esteem is the very foundation for the way they become mistreated.

This lesson took me over 40 years to learn. However back then, I didn't know any better. I actually really liked Gus and even began falling in love with him after dating for about eight months or so. I blurted it out one day as we were lying in bed. "I love you."

"I love you too, my little Nancy," said Gus tenderly. He was very nice and kind most of the time.

Not long thereafter, Gus was called upon to return to the United States for a new assignment. He had already served in Udon for a year and a half, so Gus was ready to return home. I didn't know what would happen to me after he left and by now I was attached to him. I couldn't imagine my life without him.

On the day he was to leave, Gus got down on one knee in the small garden outside of my apartment. The trees were blowing gently and the smell of Hibiscus filled the air. His blond hair gleamed bright in the sunshine and his blue eyes looked up at my face.

As he opened a small velvet box, Gus asked; "Will you marry me, Nancy? Will you come and live with me in America?" A sparkling ring twinkled its favor at me with alluring wonder.

For a second I was dumbfounded. "You don't want to marry me. I'm a call girl."

"No, you're not. You have proven not to be. You have been a faithful, good girl ever since we started dating. I'm not going to hold your past actions against you," said Gus.

"Then, YES!!" I squealed in delight as I jumped up and down and wrapped my arms around Gus's strong shoulders. "It would be my dream come true!"

"That's what I like to hear," he said, relieved by my answer. "Don't worry Nancy, I promise I will always take care of you forever."

We kissed, and then he had to leave to catch his plane to the Hill Air force Base in Utah. Right before he left, Gus and I signed fiancé papers so that he could send for me to marry him in the United States. The names on the paperwork made everything official so that he could expedite the process and meet up with me in the U.S. after the paperwork was filed.

I was to become Mrs. Gus Harvey West, the wife of a United States Lieutenant for the US Air Force. Destiny was about to be fulfilled as I had promised my mother would be done. By marrying an American man, I was certain that my path to wealth, fame and fortune was finally going to be possible.

More than anything, I wanted to fulfill my dream and promise to my mother to marry an American man and come back for her one day. I wanted to build her a big house.

My life in Thailand would be left behind, without even

time to visit my family before leaving. I waited patiently in Udon after Gus flew out. The paperwork only took a couple of weeks to arrive. By then, I really missed Gus and could not wait to see him when I arrived in Utah from the long flight overseas. He sent a plane ticket for me, as promised.

As I boarded the magnificent Lockheed C-5 Galaxy aircraft destined for the USA, I was so excited I could barely contain myself. I was finally getting out of Thailand and was determined to be the very best housewife to Gus that I could be. My chance for escape had finally arrived and I could not have been more overjoyed, such as a child on Christmas Eve as I anticipated the joy of the next day.

I packed everything I needed within one set of luggage and the rest I gave to one of the girls I worked with. She seemed glad to have it and even a little envious that I was "getting out" of the lifestyle we were subjected to.

On the redeye flight to America, I stared dreamily at the engagement ring Gus had given me. It sparkled beautifully, just like the future that was waiting for me on the other side of the Pacific Ocean.

I HAD OFTEN DREAMED OF SNOW AS A YOUNG girl, even though I had never seen it before because of the climate in Thailand. The fluffy snowflakes were something I had always imagined as being peaceful and fun.

So when the big airplane landed in Salt Lake City, Utah and I saw snow on the ground for the first time, I was instantly amazed, bedazzled and ecstatic. Everything was falling into place for me.

Gus was there to pick me up at the airport. He looked handsome in his regular street clothes. I was used to seeing him dressed in uniform or in Air Force attire, so although he looked just as handsome in his dressed blues; it was definitely a bright sight to see him wearing casual attire.

Gus greeted me with a giant bear hug and picked me up and spun me around. "Welcome to America, honey!" He presented me with a bouquet of lilies. We kissed for what seemed like an eternity.

As we drove away, it was a different feeling being in a new

country. In Udon we had walked or taken taxis everywhere. Now Gus was driving his own car as I sat proudly by his side in a strange land. Plus we didn't have the interpreter with us anymore, so our language barrier was a bit awkward. It was my silent vow to learn English now that I had finally made my way to America.

"Everything okay, princess?" he asked as he reached for my hand and set it on his lap. The engagement ring glistened as it picked up the sun's rays through the windshield.

I nodded. My eyes were big as I looked around at this new place, with foreign trees and expansive fields filled with white snow. Gus read my mind.

"It'll be a bit of an adjustment, but I promise everything is going to be alright. Stick with me and we'll go places, Babe," Gus said with a wink of reassurance. I nodded, still uncertain.

We parked and got out of the car. "Close your eyes!" Gus said as he came around to open my car door. "I have a surprise for you!"

He led me up a couple of stairs and opened a door as I tightly locked my eyelids. "Okay, open your eyes, Nancy!" he instructed.

When I did open them, I saw a beautiful room with simple, yet tasteful furnishings. "This is our new place, just for you and me," he explained proudly.

"I love it," I said as I looked around and then looked at him.

Kiddingly, I said; "The only thing it needs is a woman's

touch." The mid-sized apartment Gus had chosen was to become our home for the next couple of years.

Our new life started right away. While Gus was at work I had to find ways to occupy myself. I was so infatuated with snow that sometimes I went sliding down hills on cardboard boxes all by myself. Glee was an emotion I had never truly experienced as a child. My childhood never belonged to me, so those moments of acting like a kid were rare. Now as a young woman instead of just a girl, I was finally able to enjoy life for the first time.

In my spare time, I did a lot of reading to learn better English. Back in 1970, there were far fewer Asian immigrants who came to the United States. Therefore, I stuck out as different whenever Gus and I went out in public. People stared at us. I felt like a foreigner. It wasn't until much later that I learned the term 'minority' but I certainly learned the meaning behind it within only a few weeks of living in the States.

Nevertheless, I was mesmerized by the environment, having gone from bustling markets to free-standing stores and restaurant chains like McDonalds. The food in America was very bland in comparison with Thai food. I grew up eating rice, hot peppers and fish sauce. The Thai people often cook with zippy spices to make dishes more flavorful, so I found the food in the United States to be very lackluster.

My solution was to cook a lot, which I enjoyed. I made Gus the most amazing dishes and was able to buy us groceries and spices. We had a wonderful time together and Gus's past behavior of infidelity faded into the background as he made the choice to be monogamous. Not because he had to, but because he wanted to. This was even better. He loved me.

Our time in Salt Lake City was the happiest I had ever been in my life. It was part of life's plan for me and I felt like the challenges I overcame were well worth the reward of making it to the land of dreams.

Our wedding was to take place in Odenville, Alabama where Gus was raised. We drove there by car only a couple of months after my arrival to the States. Gus really wanted me to get an ID and a Green Card, so our plan was to get married soon.

His family still lived in Odenville, a tiny town of just over a thousand inhabitants. It was a wholesome community, the kind of place that everybody knows everybody and neighbors still knock on each other's door to borrow an egg or a cup of sugar.

Needless to say, in the rural Southern communities of backwoods Alabama, many residents had never laid eyes on Asian people before. There was no one there who looked like me, with my dark complexion and almond shaped eyes. It was rustic there, even somewhat Hillybilly-ish, if that's even a word.

I was really nervous to meet Gus's family, knowing they would look at me as being very different from the girls that

Gus had dated in the past. Like me, Gus was anxious as a teenager to escape the environment in which he was raised. That was something we had in common. Small town life got on his nerves, he often said.

That's one of the reasons why Gus had enrolled in the US Air Force. To Alice and Harvey West's chagrin, their son had met one of the Thai girls (*me*) and invited her back to the US. It was often frowned upon in that era to produce offspring with people of another skin color. Many old-fashioned Southern parents feared becoming grandparents to kids of colored races. They worried that their grandchildren would be ridiculed and perceived as half-breeds. It was an out-of-date way of thinking.

At the time I was only seventeen, still so young and naïve. Gus's parents and grandparents seemed warm and friendly enough, although the rest of his family revealed their disappointment with cordial shortness and backhanded complements.

It was clear that Gus's younger sister, Peggy, did not like me at all, despite my attempts to befriend her. Apparently she was still good friends with one of Gus's old flames, a girl he had dated back in high school. I often caught Peggy glaring at me over Gus's shoulder, even though I just tried to smile and brush it off. I had trouble speaking English, although I was getting better. Peggy had a crooked smirk every time I tried to speak to her, as if my appearance and strange accent were despicable.

There wasn't a lot of time to plan the wedding. Gus's Uncle

was to have the honor of marrying us in the backyard under a trellis. With only a couple of weeks to prepare, the invitations were limited to immediate family only, along with two of Gus's childhood pals and their girlfriends. It was to be more or less just a family get-together with a nice dinner after the ceremony.

I went shopping for a wedding gown with Gus's mother, Alice. She was very nice to me. I think she realized I was a nice person and not just a girl who wanted to marry Gus for a ticket to the United States.

During the week before the wedding, I spent time getting to know the family of my soon-to-be husband. They taught me how to shoot a gun in the backyard, using hay bales as target practice. They lived on a farm, so I helped them milk the cows and feed the goats while I was there. His parents realized that I was a hard worker and more than willing to lend a helping hand. I also really enjoyed doing it for the sake of helping the family.

Mr. and Mrs. West came to like me so much that they gave me a very generous wedding gift. To my delight, one morning I was called out into the front yard early in the morning by Harvey, Gus's father. "Nancy! Nancy!" I heard him yelling through the window. "You better git yer little Asian ass down here cuz I got a surprise for ya!"

There he was, standing in the driveway with a keychain dangling on his pointer finger. "Here ya go, Nancy. You're gonna need yer own set 'o wheels," said Harvey as he proudly revealed an orange 1963 Dodge 5 speed. This 13-year old automobile was to become a good first car for me to learn how to drive.

"Thank you, so much!" I said, tearfully. "No one has ever done such a thing for me before. I am truly grateful, Sir!"

"No need to call me Sir, Nancy. We're not too fancy 'round here," his father said with a pat to my head. Standing at about six feet tall just like his son, Harvey must have thought I was a pint-sized little kid.

For the entire morning, Harvey, Gus and I drove around the back roads of Alabama. It was fun to drive. Suddenly I felt more independent and realized what America was all about. I was so grateful to be in a country where people had the free will and means to do as they wished.

The church where we were married was very quaint and small, only holding about 30 people. On the day of the wedding, I was very nervous. We had gone through the rehearsal the night before, but the jitters still came to me on the day I was to face my husband-to-be. Alice made mimosas and Peggy sat crossly on a hope chest at the end of the bed where I prepared, slipping on my dress.

"You look so lovely, soon-to-be daughter in law!" beamed Alice. "I am so proud of you and Gus. We are happy to have you in the family."

"Oh, thank you and I'm so happy to be here," I replied. Peggy's eyes gave away her disapproval.

"Gus should've married Margie! She is the love of his

life!" she blurted out. Shocked, I looked at her in disbelief, not knowing how to react.

"Peggy!" exclaimed Alice. "How can you say such a thing? You need to accept the fact that your brother is marrying Nancy today. Apologize at once!"

"I will not!" Peggy yelled, rushing out of the room.

Alice grabbed my hands in hers, seeing the tears well up in my eyes. "Just ignore her, she will get over this in due time."

I shrugged, as I continued to prepare for the ceremony which was due to take place in only twenty minutes. I hoped I could recover from the new wave of anxiety that Peggy's outburst had stirred within my gut.

The ceremony was quick and easy, almost whizzing by in minutes that seemed like seconds. Gus's Uncle Chuck was funny but I still struggled with understanding English, so whenever he cracked a joke I just laughed when everyone else did. I hoped that no one suspected my lack of understanding. At least I knew that I was expected to say; "I do."

After the brief ceremony, a lightly decorated dinner was set up within the West farmhouse. Our simple reception décor consisted of a few balloons and a wildflower centerpiece on a long table.

The week prior, we had eaten all the normal Southern home-style dishes you can imagine. Pot roast, meatloaf, bacon and eggs, grits and cornbread. Since I had not eaten all day, I was very hungry. I was especially hungry for Thai food, since I had not had any ever since leaving Udon. My gracious husband knew this and had arranged for Thai food to be brought in from a catering company out of Columbus, Georgia, which was roughly 150 miles away.

Suffice it to say, this meal was very special and I was even more delighted to eat Thai food on our wedding day. What a thoughtful wedding gift on behalf of my new husband!

As I looked up and down the table at my wedding guests, I smiled, thinking how lucky I was to be part of a new family. Alice and Harvey, as well as his grandparents, good friends and five brothers and sisters were all there. Gus was the eldest and the younger kids all looked up to him. He was the one who had gone away in the war and became a fearless soldier. He had gone on a big adventure and had worldly stories to tell. And now, he even had a brand new wife who was a foreign reminder of his travels. Gus brought excitement to the family, to say the least.

The dinner was especially beautiful on Alice's fine china, which was an heirloom passed down to her by her great-great grandmother. She only brought it out on special occasions, so it was an honor to have her use it for our wedding meal. As we began dining, Gus's father made a quick speech and everyone began eating. Including me. I took a few bites of the delicious Thai food and savored its spicy aroma.

Suddenly, I sat up out of my chair, horrified. In the midst of eating, talking, listening and enjoying my wedding day, I had inadvertently stuck my fork in what looked like a giant white ball. It was flaky and smelled atrocious, like a foul chemical used for cleaning. Fortunately, there were no bites missing.

As I looked around nonchalantly, no one else had a white ball on their plates. Something that smelled so bad could not possibly be part of the cuisine. This was no dessert creampuff sitting on my plate.

Someone had placed rat poison in my food. On my wedding day, no less. As I looked around, I could not pinpoint anyone. Who had the audacity? Who in Gus's family disliked me so much that they would attempt to kill me with my own food, the Thai food I had longed for and that Gus had specially-ordered?

Who, and why? I jabbed Gus with my elbow. "Look!" I said loudly.

"What is this?" he asked, standing up. He smelled it.

"I don't know. Nobody else has one, I said looking around.

Gus smelled the vile ball. "I think they use this to kill the rats in the barn. I'm not sure how it ended up in your dish, honey." He immediately looked up and down the table at all of the guests, with an expression of anger.

All of the dinners had to be thrown away. Once the rat poison was discovered, everyone lost their appetites. Even the person who had done it threw away their food too, in order not to be considered a suspect. To this day, I'm still uncertain who tried to poison my food. However, I do know that it was meant for me because I did not see any other suspicious white balls in any of the other dishes.

THE QUEST FOR SERENDIPITY

Alas, the wedding reception was ruined. After that, I felt unwelcome so we left soon thereafter. My husband's parents were sympathetic and apologetic. I ruled them out as suspects as we left the family farm on our return drive back to Utah.

For now, the new car my husband's parents had given me would have to stay behind. Nevertheless, we were now officially joined as man and wife.

Chapter

10

AFTER LIVING IN SALT LAKE CITY FOR A couple of years, Gus and I moved to Hulbert Field in Florida. While there I went to school to learn English and other subjects, while also working at a little gift shop. My English speaking and understanding greatly improved and I felt more confident in my delivery. Most importantly, I was able to earn money and make friends instead of relying solely on my husband.

My main goal of course was to get my mother out of Thailand one day. I had promised her a house and a good life, one much better than what she knew from living in poverty. Fortunately I was able to stow away most of the money I made working at the gift store to save up for my mother's escape. I wrote her letters once a month and she always responded. Within each letter, I told her how wonderful America was and how we no longer had to walk everywhere. We always drove. I even bragged about the car Gus's parents had given me as a wedding present. We missed each other. Such is the bond of a mother and daughter that no distance can divide.

Gus made good money with the military and was a good provider. Our life together during those first few years of marriage was pleasant and we enjoyed one another.

Things didn't change until he came home one day to tell me that he had been offered a new assignment overseas.

"Where?" I asked, as I sat for a moment under a palm tree in our front yard.

"We can go to the Philippines if you want," Gus said without much emotion. "I know you want to be closer to your mother, so if it makes you happy then I will take the job there."

Trying not to act too excited, I said, "Yes, Gus! Let's go there and we can visit my family. You are a good husband."

So, we packed and within two weeks we left behind our belongings with Gus's family after visiting them one last time in Alabama. We left our automobiles and some of our furniture and stayed only a few short days.

Once in the Philippines, the atmosphere was entirely different. We were stationed at Clark Air Force Base and there was nothing else to do there except party. The boom in the military led to increased crime and prostitution. It was something I had not anticipated. In hindsight, I would have discouraged our transfer instead of encouraging it to happen. This was one of those 'if onlys' of life that people often learn after things transpire.

The atmosphere of Angeles City in the Philippines became one of the most urbanized military bases in the world during its time. It had every sordid temptation you can imagine, including a Red Light District and three giant servicemen's clubs, numerous bars and other less than wholesome forms of entertainment.

As a result, the relationship between Gus and I took a turn for the worse. We were happy in America and he had always been faithful. However, the environment of the Philippine lifestyle was much different and he sadly regressed to his old ways of misbehavior, just like before we were married. When we were courting in Thailand, Gus had been able to keep an 'open relationship' established with me and at the time I had been more accepting of it because I was only 16 and it was my first real relationship. Now that I knew better and had seen the way a marriage is supposed to be honored with faithfulness, I was less tolerant and far angrier when he decided to step out on me. Fights broke out between us weekly, usually over his indiscretions.

As they say, "*Idle time is the devil's playground*". Gus had too much time on his hands; therefore he spent much of it partying with new friends he made while working on the base. I partied too, but mostly just in spite of him. An eye for an eye, so to speak. So we cheated on each other. Our relationship was on and off, as we sometimes separated for a few days or weeks after a huge blowout.

I hung on to Gus at that point mostly because of the promise I had made to my mother. My mission had not yet been accomplished; therefore I needed Gus to fulfill my dream of getting her out of Thailand. In a way, I felt like I owed him so I blocked out whatever he did wrong and just accepted it quietly. Deep down, I also hoped he would come to his senses and just love me again like he had for the years we lived in the U.S.

So, instead of leaving him, I did things to better myself as a person. I exercised and took care of myself, always making sure I wore makeup and looked attractive for him daily. I kept working hard and saved as much money as I could. Going to computer school and furthering my education was another one of the military opportunities I took advantage of. Eventually I learned better English and even earned a GED. Since I spent so much time working in the fields as a child, I had missed out on the normal advantages of childhood, like graduating from high school.

Living in the Philippines was a horrible time in my life and for our marriage. Gus had been so wonderful and such a good husband when we lived in America. He truly loved me then. In fact, we grew to love each other and at that point he was a really wonderful husband. I'm not sure why the move changed all of that and it was a transition that threw me off guard.

Gus also became physically violent to me sometimes while living there. I could blame the alcohol, I suppose. He always had that mean streak somewhere inside of him. He had slapped me around a couple of times in Thailand while we were dating and before we got married, but the whole time we lived in the States he showed no signs of physicality. He never laid a hand on me, nor did he ever have a reason to want to. I wished we had stayed in Florida. Perhaps things would have remained blissful as they were in those first three or four years of our marriage. At times I even blamed myself for wanting to transfer there and be closer to my mother. Had I not said 'Yes' everything would still be fine.

Partying amplified his abusive ways. Gus liked to go out with a certain group of guys and they often left me behind to party for days straight. They drank. They did drugs. It was like reliving my childhood all over again, when my father came home after partying and gambling for days straight and fought with my mother over his own infidelities and drunken behavior.

Not only did Gus develop a lack of empathy, he had a vengefulness about his attitude. It felt like he was angry that I had encouraged us to live there, when in truth I just wanted to be closer to my mother.

Once I had finally saved up enough money, I asked my Mom if she would like to come live with us at Clark Air Force Base. She surprised me by saying no. She couldn't leave my father, she wrote in a letter. She wasn't willing to leave my Dad by himself.

So instead I used the money to buy a duplex in Thailand for my family. My mother, father and sister, Penny – who was now in her teens – would all live there. My whole family was thrilled, after having lived in a shanty for most of their lives. The duplex was like a step into a life of luxury by comparison. Both of my parents were so proud, even my Dad. We had never been close, but he was touched by my generosity and was sincerely grateful. It was one of the few moments I shared with him as an adult that was actually special. My mother cried with glee and my sister jumped up and down as I handed them the key upon a visit that Gus and I made to Thailand.

All the while, my mother stayed by my father's side until the day he took his very last breath. They had never been apart and there was nobody to take care of him. Ultimately, a life of alcoholism took its toll on my father and captured his soul at a relatively young age. It was only after his passing that she finally agreed to come live with me and Gus, but even then her request was met with yet another stipulation.

"I won't come unless your sister does, too," my mother told me. I believed her excuses were in part due to the fear of change, having lived in Thailand her whole life she knew of nothing different. She was afraid of the unknown and the life she would leave behind, even though up until that point it had not been a life filled with much joy or peace. In a way, she didn't know any better than to spend her entire life in codependency.

Undeterred, I accepted my mother's request and complied. I worked even harder so that I could bring not only my mother, but my sister Penny, as well.

After living in my intolerable marriage for a couple of

years in the Philippines, another surprise made its way into my life. I was 24 when I learned that I was pregnant. Although I did not get pregnant on purpose, Gus and I had never used protection throughout our marriage. So, I guess we were both under the assumption after seven years of marriage that I could not get pregnant. We were both wrong.

The news of becoming a father did not deter Gus's behavior. He continued partying and treated me badly. Subconsciously I hated him a little more each day, especially after he struck me even while I was with child. Even though I felt embarrassed that I had allowed myself to become a victim, I still felt helpless and insecure. I didn't know what to do to save myself and my unborn baby. If I divorced him, then Gus could have sent me back to Thailand. That was not where I wanted to be, ever again. And since we were living in the Philippines at the time of my pregnancy, my child would not have been born on U.S. soil. Therefore, I had no choice but to stay and wait it out until something changed. Gus knew this and used my helplessness against me. It was a feeling I hated and one that made me want all the more to break free in a spirit of independence. I still longed to fulfill my dreams one day.

A few nights before I was to give birth, Gus's squadron went out partying for a few nights. My husband did not come home and I was afraid of being all alone and not having someone to call upon if I were to go into labor. I felt contractions so I knew the day was nearing.

THE QUEST FOR SERENDIPITY

After the third night I grew worried. It was the day after Christmas and Gus had not even made an appearance to bring a gift the day before to celebrate Christmas with his wife. So I spent Christmas Eve with a few friends. However, Christmas Day was spent crying alone, all by myself.

Finally, I couldn't stand the anxiety anymore and went looking for him. Walking nine months pregnant to the Bilibago Entertainment District was mortifying

There was a local hangout that many of the military men frequented called '*Forbidden City*'. Cautiously, I walked in feeling terribly out of place since I was due to have my baby any day. The last place I wanted to have a baby was in a nightclub. That was certain. On my small framed body, my baby took up much of the space on my lower half and it was even difficult to walk without becoming short of breath.

People stared at me as I walked in timidly to the establishment. There were many soldiers there drinking and the local Philippine women were all dressed scantily, some of them in groups or individually with the men who visited there. I suspected some of the girls were prostitutes.

I heard Gus's familiar bellow of laughter from a corner near the back of the bar. He was gathered around a billiard table with a few other members of his unit. They were heavily engrossed in a game of pool. All were drunk. At first I just observed him, wondering if I should approach. But then I saw a woman with heavy makeup slide over next to him as Gus was just about ready to take his next shot. She ran her fingernail up the length of the pool stick flirtatiously, smiling. He smiled back at her and said, "Pooh, you're blocking my shot, sweetheart."

Infuriated, it was apparent that Gus and his buddies were there with some of the local women and that he had probably been staying with her for the last few nights, since he had not come home. I could not resist the urge by then to approach.

I walked up to the billiard table with anger in my eyes, as a tear rolled down my cheek. "What are you doing here, with her?" I yelled at Gus, then pointing to the slutty girl by his side. "I'm about to have your baby any day!"

"What the fuck are you doing here?" he said, nearly spitting his words at me in disgust.

"I've been waiting for you at home. You missed Christmas!" I said, now with more tears rolling down my face. I put my face in my hands and shook my head from side to side.

"It's none of your business. I don't want you here," said my drunken husband. "Go on. GIT!"

"I need you... the baby is coming," I replied hysterically.

"Well I said GIT! I'll come back when I'm good 'n ready and it sure as hell ain't right now!" Gus stammered in a drunken loud voice. "Don't make me tell you again!"

His friends looked on curiously at our marital dispute. I froze; my legs simply wouldn't go anywhere. I didn't want to leave, even though I wished to be anywhere but there.

Gus came around the table and lifted up his hand, angrily. "What did I say? Why don't you ever listen?"

I cowered a little bit, "Please Gus... the baby..." I pleaded, holding my stomach with one hand and with the other near my face, wincing.

His anger boiled through his drunkenness. I think he was high on drugs, too but I couldn't be certain. He grabbed my shoulders and shook me, with all of his friends watching.

"YOU WILL DO AS I SAY!" he said roughly and abruptly. Then he bunched up his fingers into a fist unexpectedly and punched me in the face. I was knocked into the table and my legs gave out from underneath me. As I fell to the floor, Gus took his position over me and slapped me several more times as I tried to protect myself with rubber arms. "You don't listen, you little bitch! I don't want you here!"

Finally one of Gus's buddies intervened. "C'mon Gus, she's pregnant... I think she's had enough." He cautiously stepped closer so that Gus could hear him. "Just leave her be."

I could barely see through all of the tears but my face was stinging and my body ached all over. Gus slapped his cue stick down on the billiard table and stomped off, most likely to the bathroom or to go outside and have a cigarette.

Someone grabbed my hand and hoisted me up off the floor. "It's not a good idea for you to be here," said one of the guys in the squadron. "You should leave, Gus is not himself today."

I limped out of the bar as everyone stared. It felt like walking through the zoo, surrounded by animals who were staring and hungry, just wanting to take a piece out of me. I couldn't leave fast enough but my body was stinging and my face was numb where my husband had hit me.

Eventually, Gus did come home the next morning. The baby was kicking steadily and I knew the labor pains would begin any moment, and they did. On December 28th my water broke and I went to the hospital. Still with a big gash on one side of my face and a couple of bruises elsewhere, a nurse asked me what had happened. "Oh, I fell down the stairs the other day," I said. "Silly me. You know my balance is off with this baby, so I'm anxious to get back on my feet." At this point I was more concerned about the painful contractions.

On December 29th my daughter came into the world. It was a joyous day. My labor lasted nearly a day, but the pain was all but forgotten the moment the hospital staff placed her on my stomach. She was beautiful. I had a lot of fears about this little newborn, the new life that I was now responsible for.

I named her Lily after my favorite flower. Motherhood was a new adjustment but I fell in love with my little infant in a way that I never imagined I would. Her little fingers and toes were so precious. She had a perfect blend of Gus and me, drawing many strong features from both of us. Her eyes had just a slight almond shape but were bigger like my husbands. Her hair was soft and brown. Lily was so cute and became my new passion. Her baby smile brought me joy despite the misery I felt around me and within my marriage. To me, the new baby was an unexpected blessing.

Gus was okay with Lily's birth. He came to the hospital with flowers, but he only stayed for a short while. He hadn't been around any babies for a long time, even though he had so many brothers and sisters. Gus didn't hold Lily very long but when he did, she smiled at him and he smiled back.

"I think she just smiled at me," he said more out loud than to anyone in particular. "You're a cute little thing."

Within a few days, I brought Lily home and my new life as a mother began. I called my mother in Thailand and we talked for a long time. She was excited to hear that I had a healthy baby girl and she seemed pleased by the name. "That is a pretty name. You will be a good Mom," my mother reassured me.

I then told her about what had happened the day after Christmas and that Gus had gone too far with his violent behavior and infidelity. I told her that I had caught him cheating on me and when I confronted him, he had beaten me up in front of everybody. At nine months pregnant, no less!

"I want to leave him, Mama," I cried. "I cannot take this anymore. He is so mean. I just can't do this!"

"You have to stay, Nuensie. You have a child to raise. You made a commitment, a sacred vow," she said.

"But what if it gets worse, what if he hurts the baby?" I asked.

My mother did not believe in divorce, which was the main reason she had put up with my father for so long. She stayed until the very end, because back in those days in Thailand it was nearly unheard of for a woman to do otherwise.

"You have to stick through this. I will be there soon to help you," my mother said. "Your father is not doing well. His health is declining."

So, that's what I did. I stayed. Once my father finally passed away, my mother was ready to come. It was not long after the baby was born. I felt a pang of sadness but there were no tears of sorrow upon my father's passing. It was better to focus on my newborn and the fact that my mother could now finally join me, as I had wanted for so long.

Gus didn't mind and seemed happy to fill out the paperwork. I think he was actually relieved that help was on its way. We promised Mom that we would try to get my sister Penny soon, but that she would have to remain in Thailand for a little while until we could work it out properly. My mother complied and waited patiently for the paperwork to pass through the military system.

It was so good seeing my mother for the first time after not seeing her for so long. It had been a couple of years since Gus and I had gone to visit and given them a key to their new home. This time, my mother was even more excited to meet her new granddaughter. She had never set foot out of Thailand and was very insecure about the new environment at first, but she adjusted well. I continued going to school while my mother helped with the baby. Naturally, she was a great blessing with the care of baby Lily.

Gus was cordial and got along well with my mother, but he still couldn't help himself from going out. Once a man has the insatiable appetite for drugs, booze and hookers, it becomes like an addiction.

Even after I had my second baby, a son, three years after my daughter was born; life in the Philippines was not ideal. My mother had been living with us for two years by the time baby Ryan was born.

Finally, the paperwork to get my sister also passed through the system so I felt like my goal of getting my family had been accomplished. Both of my children were born in the Philippines and my mother and sister had both arrived.

During the remainder of the time we all lived there, I continued attending school and doing community work. I still prayed and dreamed every day of becoming famous. Even after my children were born I kept exercising and even entered in a couple of beauty contests. Landing third place made me feel great among so many beautiful participants. *"Maybe I could become a model for the military stores,"* I thought to myself.

At the time I was also working in the TV advertising department at the military base, just so that I could be closer to my dream. Anytime I had a chance to volunteer for any kind of modeling I seized the opportunity. My quest for serendipity never died, even though by now I was in my mid twenties with two babies. In my gut, I just knew that someday my fortune would happen. I just knew it.

Chapter

11

LIVING IN THE PHILIPPINES WAS BITTER-sweet. Bitter because of the misery it had caused my marriage, but sweet because of the two beautiful children I now had who were born there, as well as finally having my mother and sister with me after so many years apart.

After living there for about five years, Gus finally got his orders for us to return to the United States. I was thrilled to hear the news and hoped that our life would go back to some stage of normalcy, at least by standards of what some people might consider normal.

We were headed for Biloxi, Mississippi at Keesler Air Force Base. Our family was bigger now, with my baby girl, infant son, my mother and of course Gus all coming. The only person who was not with us was my little sister, who had to stay behind in the Philippines because her Visa did not arrive. Somebody stole her Visa in transit. The culprit faked her name and used it to go to the U.S. with. We all felt bad but we could not stay and wait for the mix-up to be reversed. So, we left her to stay with one of my friends in the Philippines and promised to do our best to get her to America as soon as possible. Not long thereafter, she got deported back to Thailand because the process of reissuing a Visa twice to the same person was indeed complicated and not one that could be fixed easily.

Nevertheless, I was very happy to be back on U.S. grounds. I felt now as if America was my home, not Thailand and certainly not the Philippines. Gus and I bought a little house in Biloxi. It was the first house we ever owned together in ten years of marriage.

The location was ideal, being only 10 or 15 minutes from the Air Force Base. Since Biloxi is situated right near the Gulf of Mexico, we were also close to the beach and several parks that we could enjoy with our family.

Our first home was a one-story three bedroom in the suburbs. It was cute, with a touch of brick and white siding gently gracing the outside. A green hedge offered a welcoming touch and my mother and I decorated the inside with colorful curtains, using satiny red and gold fabric that reminded us of Thailand.

My daughter started preschool in Biloxi and my son was just a toddler. Gus became a better father and husband, most likely because there were no women in Biloxi to run around with and the lifestyle was more conducive to having a family. We were happy again, although we both worked a lot. His past bad habits and indiscretions once again faded into the background. I was grateful to him for bringing us back to the U.S. and for what he did to help me bring my mother home with us. Aside from his one bad habit of going out and partying and messing around, Gus was very supportive as a husband and provider. He always made sure to take care of me and our family. For that I was always grateful.

The news of my mother getting liver cancer was something I was not prepared for. She was not feeling well after about a year of us living in Biloxi. Gus was working two jobs because we struggled to make ends meet, having a family of five and a house payment to manage. Because I worked a lot too, my mother was a big help to us with the children.

Things changed after she got diagnosed. Thankfully, the military benefits helped to pay for her care but it was still not enough to meet the mounds of financial obligations. I knew I had to work even more and also try to manage taking care of her. Once the cancer treatments began, the radiation had a grave effect on her condition and my mother became very, very ill.

Meanwhile, Gus came home one day with more unexpected news. "The Air Force is transferring us to Colorado," he said.

I looked at him, blankly. "What? But we've only been here for about a year. Why?"

"Well, because they need me," he said matter-of-factly.

"But, we just bought a house here," I protested.

"Well, we'll have to sell it," he said.

"I can't leave here, I have a job working for the government and you know my mother is sick," I replied.

"Nancy, you know how this works. You married a military man. You never know when Uncle Sam is going to send us somewhere new. That's just the way it is," said Gus.

"And our daughter started school here. And my mother's cancer ... we can't just switch all of her doctors and move her in the midst of all this, what if she doesn't make it?" I tried my best to rebut.

"I'll have to go without you, then," said Gus. "I'll come back to visit whenever I get weeks off."

I knew that would not be often. The men on duty sometimes got a week off once a month. Nevertheless, Gus left us behind and went to Colorado by himself.

Things became even more difficult when he left. Because we still had our mortgage to pay for and now he had to pay rent in Colorado, our income went from 'just keeping afloat' to 'barely drowning' with too many bills and not enough money coming in.

Feeling like a cat dangling on a rope with just claws hanging on for dear life, I took on yet another job. One job paid $2.75 an hour working at a gas station. Another subservient job at Keesler Air Force Base paid only $5.00 an hour, working at the small BX store. The third job was as a secretary assistant for military housing, also at the AFB. Between working three jobs and taking care of my sick mother, I barely saw my children.

My husband made enough money to take care of us but not enough to pay bills. Because we lived in two different states, the expenses were greater. For awhile he did send money to help us, although it was infrequent and not really enough to pay for anything substantial.

I had a babysitter for the children, especially for my son who was now a toddler and walking. My daughter just started school and was becoming old enough to help out more, but certainly she was not self-sufficient or reliable enough to manage on her own.

One day Lily waited up for me as I returned home, exhausted from working three jobs.

"Mommy, we miss you," Lily said in her sweetest little girl voice. "I wish you didn't have to work so much."

"Me too, sweetheart. How was your day?"

"Claudia hit me today," said Lily.

"WHAT?!" I said, looking shocked. Claudia was the babysitter.

"She said I said a bad word," Lily said as she looked down.

I stood up, infuriated. I called up Claudia and immediately fired her, despite her denying the story and stating that Lily was only making such things up because she wanted me to spend more time at home. As far as I was concerned, you could never be too careful when it came to who you left your child with.

The only godsend I had was a close friend named Dee,

who also happened to be my boss at one of the three jobs. She knew I was all alone with the kids and that my mother had cancer. She knew that Gus had gone to Colorado and left me with a mortgage payment and two little mouths to feed. So, Dee looked after my children for me while I was at work during the day, especially my son who wasn't yet in school. Dee cared for them and even cooked food for the kids and for my mother. After having chemotherapy and great suffering with the cancer, my mother was in no condition to feel like making dinner, much less eating it sometimes.

Dee was an angel and genuinely cared about us. She picked my daughter up at school some days and took my son to his doctor's visits on others. She was a help spiritually, financially and mentally – a blessing to us all. Dee was most appreciated by me and remained one of my truest friends throughout the years.

Life was hard. Gus never visited, not even once after he moved to Colorado. In fact, he stopped sending money and even stopped calling after only a few months. I was so busy working that I tried to push my feelings of abandonment off to the side, but inside something told me that things had gone awry.

My feelings were right. I finally got through to Gus one day on a Sunday afternoon. I had left him a couple of messages only days prior, but he had not returned my phone calls.

I dialed again, expecting to hear his voice on the other end, even if it was the answering machine. However, I was extremely surprised when I heard the voice of a woman who answered instead.

"Hello, who is this?" I asked. "I must have misdialed. I was looking for Gus."

"No, this is Gus's house. Who is this?" asked the woman.

"His wife." I said it coldly, feeling my blood tingle as my arms went numb with anxiety. "Is he there?"

"Ya. But he's in the shower. I'll tell him you called," the woman said, hanging up abruptly.

I stared at the receiver in disbelief. *Who could this be? Why did a woman answer the phone?* I could only assume he had gone back to his old ways. His partying... his promiscuity... his polished misbehavior.

Gus called back after about twenty minutes. "Hi Nancy. Before you grill me, hear me out."

"You bastard!" I interrupted. "How could you do this to me? To our kids? To our family?"

"Do what? You don't know Nancy," he paused.

"Do what you're doing, that's what. I know all about it. Out partying, drinking and picking up hookers, just like you did in the Philippines!" I yelled across the line.

"No, I'm not, actually," he said calmly. "It's not like that."

I was confused by his calm state. In the past when we had argued about him going behind my back with other women, Gus always yelled and defended his actions.

"Nancy, I'm sorry," he said almost with an air of condolence, "I've met someone else."

I was silent for a moment. Stunned. "Who? Who is she?"

"Her name is Susan. We've been dating each other for a few weeks," he explained. "I'm sorry, I wanted to tell you sooner but there hasn't been any time."

"That's bullshit!" I screamed.

"Nancy, it's your fault anyway. I think you have been cheating on me ever since I left. You're never there when I call," he said, turning the blame to me.

"How dare you! I'm never here because I'm working at three jobs to pay for this house and our kids! My mother is dying for Chrissake, Gus!" I spat angrily into the receiver. "I'm not cheating, nor do I have the time. How dare you turn this on me? Just because you can't keep your dick in your pants it's all my fault, isn't that right, Gus?"

"Look, we can do this civilly or we can do battle, it's your choice," he said without emotion. "I'm with Susan now."

"Unbelievable! ..." I said, however I didn't have a chance to finish. Gus interrupted.

"We can make things easier for you. I'm going to come get the kids," he said as if I didn't have a say in the matter.

"Over my dead body!" I said. I couldn't believe what I was hearing. "I raised these kids, you didn't."

"Well I can see we're not going to be civil about this. The kids are coming to live with me. I hired an attorney," he said, matter-of-factly.

I slammed the phone down into the cradle, so loudly that it scared the children. My son started screaming as he saw tears stream down my cheeks. He rarely had witnessed his mother crying and it was enough to make him upset. "Ma ma!" he screamed with outstretched arms.

I held both children tightly in both of my arms. "No one is taking my babies. Nobody!" I said fearfully. I called out sick from work for the rest of the day and hid in my bedroom, crying and staring at the ceiling in bewilderment.

Gus had done a lot of things, but I never imagined him leaving me for another woman. '*I should have gone to Colorado with him and this would never have happened*,' I thought to myself. '*How dare he? How could he?*'

My life was crumbling like stale crackers, right before my very eyes. At that moment I felt hopeless. Everything was about to become one big blur.

Chapter

12

THE LOUD KNOCK ON MY DOOR STARTLED me. No one ever came to our house at 7:00 a.m. in the morning; it was too early for most salespeople. Even the neighbors were still sleeping at that hour. I peeked around the corner through the sheer curtains and saw a man standing on the front stoop. He was fidgeting with his tie, waiting for the door to open.

"Can I help you?" I asked through the door.

"I'm here to see Nuensie Suku. Is she here?" the man asked, professionally.

"What is this in regard to?" I said, not wanting to open the door.

"Ma'am, I have important papers that I have been asked to deliver to you by Lieutenant Gus Harvey West," he said.

I opened the door for him. It was Friday the 13th of June, 1986. Even though I wasn't superstitious, in retrospect it seemed like a fitting day for the tornado of fury that my life was about to become.

As soon as I opened the door, the gentleman pulled out a

pen. "I need you to sign here," he said pointing at a line on the formal-looking document.

"Sign for what? What am I signing?" I asked inquisitively.

"Ms. Suku, you are being served. The papers will give you instructions for court proceedings that are to take place in two weeks. These are from your husband," he explained.

I couldn't imagine he was already filing for divorce. The sting of him leaving me for someone else was still fresh and the blister had far from healed.

"I'm sorry, Ms. Suku," he said. "I am just doing my job." I nodded, courteously.

Standing at the door in awe, I signed and took the papers from him. As he turned and retreated towards his car, I was dumbfounded.

Inside its contents were indeed papers from my husband, but they were not divorce papers. He was filing for custody of Lily and Ryan. I was devastated.

With only two weeks to prepare, I didn't know what to do. I wasn't familiar with the court system and could barely afford to live, much less hire a lawyer.

To make matters worse, my mother's health was declining severely. She was barely hanging on by a thread and had lost so much weight. It was her desire to go back to Thailand to finish out her time here on earth, where she was born and raised and spent so much of her life. It was where she wanted to die.

Mother was lying on the couch and looked so frail. She could barely move some days. I went upstairs and looked at my precious babies, still sleeping. Lily sensed my presence and her eyes opened a little.

"Good morning sunshine," I whispered. She smiled. She had no idea what was going on between her father and I. All she knew was that he was gone away to work for awhile.

Over the next two weeks I tried to spend as many precious moments with my kids as I could, but working at three jobs did not make it easy. I didn't really know what to do to prepare for court. Since I couldn't afford a lawyer, I hoped the judge would favor the children staying with their mother, where they belonged. They were my children and I didn't want to lose them. Honestly, the kids were my main reason for living.

Unfortunately, Gus had gone through the military court system. It was smart on his part but it worked against me in the fight for custody of my kids. Biloxi, Mississippi was a very racist community in a way, even in the 80's. Especially the court system highly favored Caucasians, not black people or Asian or any immigrants from outside of the U.S.

The judge was swift to make his decision. I was up against Gus and Susan who stood nicely dressed next to their high-powered attorney. I stood alone.

For the first time I got a glimpse of the woman Gus had left me for. I had imagined her as a drop-dead gorgeous supermodel and was expecting a Barbie doll type of girl. However, I was surprised to see that Susan was just an average girl.

She had shoulder-length brown hair with a few blonde highlights. She was taller than me, perhaps about 5'7" or so. She was 'busty' but not fat. Her eyebrows came together with a cross expression, but maybe that was because of the circumstances. Susan was just a plain-looking girl with no real defining or unique characteristics.

I couldn't figure out why Gus had left me for her, except that deep down I realized we were both unhappy so maybe he was looking for any way of escape. Our miseries in the Philippines had taken their toll our marriage. Unfortunately this dilemma was about to affect our kids – in a big way – and one that would put a strain in my relationship with them for a lifetime.

"I hereby award full custody of Lily and Ryan West to their father, Gus Harvey West. Mrs. Nuensie Suku, the children's mother, will have visitation rights. It shall be determined in another hearing as to whether she will be responsible for child support payments."

I heard the judge say it, but I couldn't believe my ears. His harsh ruling snapped me out of the daze I was in as I studied Susan and Gus together. "Your honor," I blurted out. "Please, that's not fair!"

He slammed the gavel on its post as if to finalize his answer. "I'm sorry, Mrs. Suku. It is in the best interest of the children."

And that was that. My kids were ordered to go with my estranged husband and his new girlfriend. They were now one big happy family. I felt more alone than ever. It felt like someone sliced my heart open and shoved it back into my chest as just an empty shell. Empty... lifeless... meaningless.

In the judge's eyes, Gus and Susan could provide the stability that I could not. Because I was working so much trying to make ends meet and pay the mortgage by myself, I was not in an ideal position such as Gus. He now had everything he wanted. I cringed, knowing Gus now had the upper hand.

They took my babies that day. It was emotionally tumultuous. My eyes hurt so badly from crying I swear they were bleeding. I could barely see. The children were upset, too. They didn't know their father all that well and at that age they wanted their Mommy. They were used to me and they loved me.

Even though Gus was supposed to let me have visitation rights, he did not. So after he took the kids, it was the last time I would see them for a long time. Not being able to hire an attorney on my behalf was a big mistake, but one that could not have been avoided. The money coming in was far less than the money going out and I was up to my eyebrows in mounds of bills.

My mother left for Thailand not long thereafter. She was barely strong enough to make the journey. My sister was there to meet her and help her through her final days on earth. We had never been able to rouse the paperwork to get Penny a new Visa after someone had stolen her identity in the Philippines so she was subsequently deported back to Thailand. Therefore, my mother's dying days would be spent with Penny.

It was only a matter of about five weeks that my mother passed away. It was September of that same year. All of the people I loved the most were gone within one year of my life. Everything I had come to America for was suddenly yanked out from underneath me. My husband, my children, my mother and all of my dreams were now in shambles.

That was not all that I lost. The bank seized my house in foreclosure due to my struggles to stay afloat. I was three months behind on my mortgage so I was notified of lis pendence. I begged the bank to work with me, but banks have no mercy when it comes to repayment. I explained my situation but I think they saw me more as a lost cause than a real person with serious problems. Plus they just had no reason to help me. They were looking for their money. Despite working three jobs, I had fallen way too far behind to make the mortgage payment on my own. Even though Gus's name was also on the note, I was the one living there so the bank mostly came after me.

Once they took my house, I truly had nothing. I had lost everything except for a few belongings. I lost the place I lived in and all of the people I loved. To say that I had fallen into a deep pit of despair would be an understatement. Hopelessness crept into my soul like an evil demon. All I wanted in the world was to see my son and daughter.

THE QUEST FOR SERENDIPITY

A friend tipped me off that Gus and Susan had moved to Florida. Since I still worked at the base, I was able to locate an address. My rights were to see my children; the judge had awarded me with visitation. It was Gus who was bucking the system by not allowing me to talk to the kids, nor to see them.

I finally got a phone number for them and called several times. I had just moved to a new apartment because the bank repossessed my house. Finally, Gus did answer after several days of me trying to reach them, although I never left a message.

When I kindly asked when I could see my children, Gus was not so cordial. "How did you get this number? No, Nancy. It's not a good idea."

It was evil of him to keep me from my children. He would not even let me speak to them on the phone. I kept trying, however the phone number changed not long thereafter. I realized the only way I would ever see my kids again was to fight back by hiring an attorney. How was I going to do that when I could barely make ends meet?

Every day was the same. Work, work, work. There was no joy in my life. There was nothing to live for. In a way I felt defeated. I couldn't comprehend not having my family and my dreams had been sucked deeply into a black hole. *'What happened to the great life I was supposed to have?'* I wondered. Some days I could barely muster the desire to crawl out of bed, as I often cried myself to sleep or drowned my troubles with a few drinks.

The day I decided to kill myself was a lonely day in autumn. The leaves were swirling as the trees became barren and cold, much like the emptiness I felt with the pain of losing everyone I had loved so much. My sister sent a letter from Thailand a few days prior to inform me of my mother's passing. Without her spirit I felt the loss of guidance that only a mother's love can bring.

Unlike many people who attempt suicide, I did not plan my actions. It was more like a negative bubble that finally burst. I did not call in sick for work, nor did I go out special to buy any tools or pills. The only thing I could find once I reached the decision to end my life was a few bottles of Tylenol.

Swallowing each pill deliberately at first, I washed them down one-by-one with a big glass of vodka. I looked in the mirror at the smeared makeup and disheveled hair caused by day's worth of crying. At that moment I felt ugly inside and out. My sad reflection in the mirror represented a lost soul; someone who had lost the greater part of their internal spirit. Still swallowing more and more pills, I began taking them by the handfuls instead of one-by-one. I hoped that my next life would fare better than this one.

As I began fading off into a coma, I thought about Gus and what he had done to me. He just didn't give a damn. He had found himself a new family and that was that. It didn't faze him one iota that his own children wanted and needed their mother. Susan was not their mother. She could never replace me.

THE QUEST FOR SERENDIPITY

To make matters worse, Susan brainwashed my children. She told them that I left them and wanted nothing to do with them. I believe that when a child hears that their mother no longer wants to be a part of their lives, it greatly affects the child's confidence and self-esteem. There is no doubt that these words greatly affected their well-being and caused them serious disappointment. Both Gus and Susan kept me away from my children. Every time I tried to contact them or visit them I was refused.

My boss was like an angel on the days when I was at my lowest point. She knew that I was a faithful employee and that I would never miss a day of work for any reason. Work was the only thing I had to live for, therefore I drowned myself with as much work as possible and managed a very busy schedule of juggling all three jobs.

I didn't hear the knock at the door when Dee came to check on me after failing to appear to work for two days. She knew something was wrong when nobody answered but did not have a key to get in, so she called the police.

The police rushed to my home and busted through the door, where they found me laying on the floor between the bathroom and the bedroom. Blood trickled from my nose and my skeleton frame barely sustained my body. I had been in a coma for two days and had lost so much weight I was down to 75 lbs.

Amazingly, I made it through the ordeal and was still alive. My time had not yet come to die and I was obviously meant to do something more... something greater. The medical professionals required that I must attend counseling, which is something standard when people make a decision to end their life. My situation was no exception.

"Why don't you find something positive to do with your time?" asked the counselor. She told me not to focus on people but instead to focus on something else. Deep down I did not want to give up on the fight to see my children.

Gus had hurt me so badly in a way that I had never been hurt before. Heartbreak is the type of pain that doesn't dissipate. Even prior to Gus, it seemed that any man with whom I came across hurt me in some way, even my own father with the pain he had caused our family. The only man who had never hurt me was Pete, the gentleman who had taken care of me after I was raped and hurt so badly.

I wanted to hurt men the way they had hurt me my whole life. I wanted to make them suffer. Thus, hating men became my new focus. I became a man hater for a spell, except the kind of man hater that uses men and then throws them to the curb.

Since I was newly single and childless, I began dating again. It boosted my self esteem to have men fawning over me and vying for my attention. I dated many men but never slept with any of them because I was too hurt from the pain of being left for another woman. It just made me feel empowered to treat men like shit so I used them and let them wine me and dine me. Still very pretty and in good shape, I was able to attract nice looking men and even had a few who were fighting over me.

Drinking was also a new theme. I drank away many of my woes because it made me forget about the pain. Every day I thought about my children, wondering how they were doing and what they looked like. Children change so much when they are toddlers and preschoolers. Their appearance, their personalities, and their demeanors change daily as they grow up so fast. I wondered if they missed me as much as I missed them and my heart longed to see them, even if it was for only one day.

One night I went out drinking with some of my friends. They were coworkers from my job at the BX. We were hoping to meet men, but mostly our goal was to dance and drink and have a good time.

Dressed to the nines, I was wearing a sexy satin fuchsia blouse that came down on one shoulder. It was the perfect accent to the hot black miniskirt and 3" pumps; some strappy sandals that made my legs look long and lean.

The Raven was a favorite dance club that we often frequented. While there I ran into one of the men I had gone out with a few times. He was just another guy whom I had discarded as soon as someone better came along. Unfortunately he didn't understand what he had done wrong, but the true answer was nothing. He meant nothing more to me than a sticky note that gets written off after the message expires.

At the same time, another man who I was talking to was also there. He bought drinks for me and even a couple of drinks for my female companions. The drinks were flowing, when all of a sudden the leftover guy became very jealous when he saw me talking to someone new. He went up to the new guy and tapped him on the shoulder. "I think you have something of mine," he said, looking straight at me.

"Beat it. She looks pretty content," the new guy replied. A fight ensued.

I looked at my girlfriends and yelled, "We've gotta go!" I was feeling pretty tipsy. None of them wanted to leave yet because they were flirting and dancing and having a great time.

So, I grabbed my things and downed another couple of shots. The men fighting over me made me feel like a piece of meat. Honestly, I didn't even like myself anymore. This was not my intent and despite my drunken stupor I could no longer handle the whole scene.

The lights spun quixotically from the disco ball along with flashes of light from the middle of the dance floor. As I watched out of the corner of my eye, a bouncer broke up the fight and forced both men to leave. My girlfriends were nowhere to be found. Most likely they were on the dance floor or in the bathroom. So I just stood on the edge of the dance floor, barely able to stand because I was so drunk.

Another strange man approached me. Men on the prowl look for drunken girls, especially the ones who get separated from the pack. Like a stray deer on the edge of a stampede in Nairobi, the man moved in like a lion moving in for the kill. Men love to find the weak ones, the drunken ones, the women who may just go home with them because they are too intoxicated to know any better.

I was not about to fall for it. Quickly, I turned in the other direction and walked straight to my car. So drunk I could barely put the key in the ignition, I started the engine and sat there for a minute. Drunk people often justify driving home by claiming they are fine. Even though I knew I was not fine, I just didn't care. I didn't care about anything anymore except about getting back to my apartment.

Unfortunately, I never made it home. The rest was just a blur.

13

"**M**OMMY, MOMMY, WAKE UP!" IN MY dream, I saw my baby boy trying to awaken me from a slumber. His beautiful brown eyes peered down at me from above my face, as his little fingers tried to pry my eyelids open.

As my eyes finally opened, I tried to adjust them in a state of unawareness and confusion. Where was I? My baby boy was nowhere to be found. It was just my imagination.

Ahead of me I could vaguely make out the figure of a giant tree. Daylight had revealed the results of a blackout from the night before. My car was smashed against a big elm tree. The whole front was crushed and the windshield was smashed. Next to me in the passenger seat there was a giant branch poking in from the right window. The dashboard was crumpled like a cardboard accordion and the steering wheel had pushed forward, nearly coming up to my chest. Somehow my seat had gone all the way back to the reclining position, which had actually saved my life. My shoes were in the backseat, although I couldn't remember if I had taken them off before leaving the club or if they had fallen off in the accident.

Miraculously, I was alive. Not only was I alive but I was virtually unscathed. I had to escape through the back of the car since the front was so badly wrecked and the door was nothing more than a piece of tin like the lid of a soup can. A little wobbly, I stood next to the debris that was once my vehicle with a dumbfounded expression. My car was completely totaled, but somehow I was still alive.

After standing there in awe for a few minutes, I looked around trying to determine where I was. Quite ironically, I had landed smack dab at the entrance of a cemetery. It was a cemetery I often drove by on my way to town, yet I had never truly noticed it until now. I shook my head in disbelief and covered my face with my hands, sobbing.

Of all the places to have crashed, somehow I landed in the cemetery. The irony of it all was what struck me the most. Just a couple of months prior I had actually tried to commit suicide. However, crashing my car while drunk driving nearly ended everything. Oh, how ironic!

Still feeling woozy from a severe hangover and bashing headache, I sat in the cemetery just staring at my car. I was still in shock as I looked at the car, wondering how my life had been spared when there was barely anything left of the whole front of the car. Even more amazing was the fact that I was able to walk away without much more than a scratch or two. To me this was a sign from a higher power... a wakeup call!

I vowed to change my ways and to adopt a new focus. Getting my children back was going to become my new goal. Still crying, I realized that the person I had become ever since losing my family was not a good person. I did not even like myself anymore. I wanted to forget everything bad that had happened in my life, from the lack of a childhood – to the rape, bad times in my marriage, divorce, and most of all – to forget the pain of losing everyone who mattered most to me. Instead I was now going to worry about me. It was an epiphany to realize that as long as I hated myself I would never be able to attract the love I so desired and longed for. Everyone deserves love.

For the moment I had to think about what to do in the immediate situation. Somehow my car had pulled its way into a cemetery with giant trees that were hundreds of years old. Of course, I didn't remember the accident. The whole thing was a blackout. In fact, I didn't even remember leaving the nightclub. My last memory was of the two men fighting over me and then bolting as fast as I could to get away from the whole scene.

Escape. That was what I needed to do. The life in Biloxi was not conducive to my good health or well-being. That day, I realized that it was time to move on into the next phase of my life.

Aching badly, I finally stood up and brushed myself off. My neck hurt and my head pounded as I tried to find my purse. Weren't there some aspirin in there somewhere? I didn't dare to call the police because I was afraid of getting a DUI. But my car was totaled and I knew I had to do something. So, I decided to wait and call it in after some time went by.

I walked a couple of miles up the road, still a bit lame from the accident and the relentless headache. The sun beat down profusely and I was so thirsty. I puked a couple of times in the ditch, but kept walking anyway. Having traveled this road many times, I knew there was a convenience store up ahead but it seemed much farther away when walking. A couple of miles seemed like ten. Especially because I felt so sick and sore.

When I finally reached the store, I used the few dollars I had left to buy a jug of water and to make change for the payphone. Then I called a male friend of mine who knew a guy that owned a tow truck business.

After calling him from a payphone, he showed up an hour later and drove me back to the scene. I begged him not to tell anyone and promised to pay him for his help. When he saw the car, he was shocked that anyone could have lived through such an accident, much less walk away from the scene with barely a scratch or a bruise.

He dropped me off at my apartment and took the car back to his junkyard. I still didn't dare to call the police and the car wasn't worth a great deal so I chalked it up to a serious lesson learned and vowed to devote my life to God or Buddha. I thanked the invisible magic of the Universe for protecting me and keeping me safe.

From that day on I worked on my self-esteem and made a promise to better my life. Instead of giving up I went to work regularly and gave up drinking altogether. I began attending church every Sunday habitually, as I had done years ago when my family brought me to the beautiful temple in Thailand. A few new friends I made there often encouraged me with their spiritual attitudes. Finally, I felt more normal and tried to do little things every day to bring on newfound happiness and internal joy.

There was still something missing though, and that was the love of my daughter and son. I missed them terribly and thought about them every minute of every day. I dreamed about them at night and imagined how wonderful it would be just to hold them, hug them, kiss them and play with them. It was my new goal to find them somehow. As they say, where there is a will there is a way and although I didn't know how it could be done, I wanted so badly to find them and rekindle our relationship.

Not long thereafter I made a decision to move on and leave Mississippi behind. The wakeup call of surviving a near fatal crash made me realize that there was something better out there waiting for me and that I was meant to be alive for some reason. Not knowing where to go, I pondered for a couple of weeks as to where I would move to and how I could find my kids. It was time to make money and change my focus to look for Ryan and Lily. Gus had hidden them well by disappearing.

THE QUEST FOR SERENDIPITY

Sadly, I said goodbye to my beloved friend Dee and my boss, both of whom had been my closest friends and wonderful angels for the duration of the painful experiences I had endured while living in Mississippi. Come to think of it, the entire years spent in Biloxi were nothing more than a black cloud of evil that had rained its wrath upon my head for weeks, months and now years.

My job transferred me to San Angelo, Texas, where I became the night manager at the front desk of a lodging facility for new military transfers. Life filled me with new hope and purpose as I moved into a sunny new apartment in a new and strange city. The people in Texas had fascinatingly strange accents and used different words than other cities I had visited or lived in.

Some of the women told me prior to moving to Texas that there were a lot of rich oilmen who lived there. My eyes filled with wonder at the hopes of meeting a rich oilman, one who would treat me like a princess and who could help me find my children.

My new job was very cool and was definitely classier than the jobs I had worked at before. I got to dress up nicely and feel pretty again. We wore sexy blue suits with sport coats and either black slacks or skirts. It was much better than the casual attire I had worn at the convenience store job.

Plus there were always handsome military men coming and going. The hotel was well equipped with modern meeting facilities so there were often big conventions and trade shows that took place there. It was a socially-inspiring atmosphere in a nice city. For the first time in a long time I was smiling again, filled with new energy and zest for living.

Unfortunately there were no rich oilmen, but there were a lot of military men who came and went. Somehow I was always attracted to military men and being right there on another popular base afforded ample opportunity to bump into yet another military man. Of course I dated a few likely candidates, but not in the same way I had recklessly used and abused the men who took me out in Mississippi. This time I was pickier and only dated men who had something to offer. It wasn't that I was looking to get married right away because I was still hurt over the pain of my husband's harsh and abrupt decision to choose someone else.

Mostly it was companionship that interested me. The men I met were educated and more sophisticated, unlike the hillbillies in Biloxi.

I took on a second job at the small BX exchange in addition to the night manager position at the lodging desk. There were a couple of new friends I made there and occasionally we went out together to have fun. Out of the handful of men I dated, there just wasn't anyone who gave me that 'ga-ga' feeling. That is, until one random day about a year and a half after living in Texas.

Jon was a brand new graduate ROTC from Mississippi. As he arrived at the front desk I greeted him with the usual charm that any woman would muster when a cute guy comes by, especially if she is single. He was tall with blonde hair and blue eyes and looked very handsome in his military blues. There was a gravitating attraction between us as we flirted and chatted for awhile. Since I was the night lodging manager, I gave him one of the best rooms we had available simply for the fact that he was good-looking and I liked him.

Even though he was only 23, Jon was a lieutenant for the Air Force and seemed like a very smart and charming man. It didn't bother me that I was older than he was by eleven years and it gave me a rush to know that such a handsome younger man was interested in me. It pumped up my confidence to have his attention.

For the next few days I found him making silly excuses to come to the front desk when I was working, just to get a chance to talk to me. A missing toothbrush or locking his key in the room were just a couple of mishaps he likely did on purpose. We were wildly attracted to each other and he made me laugh with his jovial, flirtatious personality.

After his week stay at the military lodging, Jon finally got clearance to be put up in his own apartment. It was typical for new recruits to stay in our lodging premises while waiting for their own place. Of course the higher commandos were given privileges beyond the rookies and usually got houses for their whole family instead of just an apartment.

Upon the day of checkout, Jon got shy on me. After flirting all week I was hoping our last day would be fun, but he seemed down. "Why the sad face?" I asked him, playfully. "Usually you're happy to see me!"

"That's just it. I wish I'd be able to see you again," he said with a coy smirk.

"Then, why don't you take me out to dinner tomorrow night?" I asked, slipping him a note with my home phone number written on the front.

He perked up, "That'd be fun." That southern Mississippi accent was one I had become familiar with over the past few years. "I'll take you to Timberville Steak House tomorrow. How's about 7:00?"

"Perfect," I said sweetly.

All through dinner the next evening, Jon couldn't take his eyes off of me. He made me melt in a way other men I had gone out with did not. Instead of looking at me as just another pretty face, he wanted to get to know me. Jon seemed intrigued and mesmerized, as I was with him also.

There was something different about him. Maybe it was the fact that I was 34 and he was only 23, even though I looked much younger than my true age. He was boyishly charming and naïve, yet in a sincere way that was quite endearing. Other men lied about things to sound better or more experienced, but Jon was real. He was just himself, a sweet guy who wanted to make me happy.

Jon didn't drink or smoke. He was a good 'ol Southern Baptist Christian lad who had never caused any harm and who would give anyone the shirt off his back. To say he was wholesome would be accurate. In fact, before joining the military he had never lived anywhere other than with his parents in a small town of Mississippi. Moving to Texas was his first experience outside of the sheltered way of life he had been living in throughout his childhood and growing up years.

We began seeing each other regularly and enjoyed a wonderful romance. I had not been with anyone in a long time because I was picky and had gone through my hating men phase prior to meeting Jon, so when the time was right and we finally made love for the first time, the feeling was wonderful. There is something of a rush when a woman in her thirties dates a man in his twenties, perhaps because of the heightened sexual compatibility.

When it finally happened our relationship became a fiery and erotic connection. The sex was insatiable and for the first time in my adulthood I learned the power of a mental and physical connection.

I told Jon more than I had ever told anyone, even my ex-husband. We had a unique connection and I felt like he tried to understand me. There was also less of a language barrier than I had experienced with my husband in the beginning, since I finally had a better grasp of the English language. Jon truly listened to and cared about me. When he heard about my history and having my children yanked away without ever seeing them again, he vowed to help me.

Knowing that I needed to have a stable relationship and

family life was vital in my efforts to find my children. It was my resilient mission not only to get my children back one day, but also just to get a chance to find them and see them again.

Therefore, I knew that I had to make this new relationship with Jon work. I felt like he was the "ONE" who would be caring towards me, as well as being a good person and a family man. He gave me butterflies like I had never felt with other men, not even my husband. For the first time in a long time, I was truly happy again.

The leave and move to San Angelo was a good move for me. And I was proud of myself for not turning back to my old ways, although I did like to go out and have fun with my friends every once in awhile and loosen up with a few drinks. I never repeated the behavior that took place in Biloxi and was not proud of the way I had handled things. Nevertheless, I had been given another chance at life so I finally seized the moment and went with my feelings.

And for the first time in my life I learned the difference of being in love, versus just loving someone. Loving someone and saying you care for them is not a deep love. With Jon it was a real love, the kind where you know the other person is thinking about you even when you're not together, rather than trying to score with other women behind your back.

Jon fell in love with me right away. I enjoyed his company and loved him too, but because I had always been hurt by men throughout my entire life, I was never able to truly let myself go with any man. My walls were high but he was able to knock them down a little more and more each day. And even though Jon loved me more than I loved him, our relationship worked and was wonderful.

After dating for about a year, Jon asked me to meet his parents. It was the next stage of any serious relationship and maybe an answer to my prayers of finally having a chance to find and get my children back. Maybe he would even marry me? I often wondered.

The only snag was Jon's parents. As devout Baptists and Southern Christians, his old-school parents wanted a traditional girl for Jon. He had gone to college and gone out with a few girls, but Jon had never dated a woman who was a little older. Certainly none who were of another race. The fact that I was "*a color*" and older than Jon was appalling to them. They wanted him to marry a solid Baptist Christian white girl.

He brought me home to them a few months before proposing, but the trip was short and sweet. Once they saw me and met me, the prejudgments were written all over their faces. The telltale scowls of disappointment were immediate.

"Jon, can we talk to you for a few minutes?" asked his parents, only a short while after we had arrived at their humble ranch home in Mississippi. It was everything you would have expected from good Christian folks in a small town, including a white picket fence and old terrier dog named Cookie, who wagged her tail in joy upon seeing Jon.

"Excuse me just a minute, sweetheart," Jon said, as he left me sitting uncomfortably on the tattered sage sofa in the family den. "I'm just going to go talk to Mom and Dad for a few minutes." He kissed my cheek and smiled. I mustered a contrived grin for them and nodded.

I could hear them faintly through the door of the pantry. "Jon, what is wrong with you?" asked his father. "We raised you better than this."

"She's wonderful," Jon defended me. "You just need to get to know her. Give her a chance!"

"She's Chinese and she looks older than you. How old is she?" asked his father.

"She's not Chinese, Dad. She's from Thailand. And she's 34, but what does it matter?" he said defensively.

"Ain't there any nice white girls in Texas to date? I've seen some mighty pretty blondes on the television programs," his Dad replied.

"And 34? Why the woman outta be ashamed of herself for going after a young man like you!" exclaimed Jon's mother. "She's robbing the cradle."

"I can't believe you two! Why can't you just be happy for me? I love her. We've only been here for twenty minutes so you've barely given her a chance," Jon said. "Just get to know her and you'll like her."

"We don't approve," they said. "She is colored. You weren't raised that way, Jon. Baptist people don't date outside of their religion. What would the church folk think?"

"Fine. I don't know why you can't be happy for me. I want you both to be part of my life. You're my family, my parents," Jon said, exasperated. "But if you can't be nice to Nancy then maybe we should just leave."

"Spend the night, at least. We haven't seen you for awhile," said Jon's mother. "She can sleep on the sofa."

"NO. I will sleep on the sofa and she can have my room," said Jon. "Then we'll leave in the morning."

As I looked around the den at all of Jon's family photographs, I could tell he had been babied by his parents. In every photograph he was the superstar of their lives, being the only child and son of Mr. and Mrs. Wakely. There were pictures of him from babyhood through his teens, college years and military graduation. Jon was the apple of their eyes.

When they came back in the room I felt incredibly uncomfortable. Not meeting their approval was disappointing.

We left the next day, not saying much on the return trip to Texas. "I'm really sorry, Nancy. You didn't do anything wrong," Jon said, patting my leg from the driver's seat as we made the journey back in his 1982 Toyota Landcruiser.

"I just wanted them to like me," I said feebly as a tear rolled down my cheek.

Jon did his best to console me. "They will, one day. It's just gonna take some getting used to for them. They're very old school. You know how older people get set in their ways?"

I thought about that moment and the entire weekend as Jon proposed to me on a hillside in San Angelo. Before I delivered the "YES" he longed to hear, I asked him about his family. "What will your family think? Won't they be upset?"

"I don't care what anyone thinks, honey. I love you and want to spend my life with you. I want to help you find your children and be a family with you, all of you," he replied, tenderly.

How could I refuse such a sincere request? I loved him and felt like Jon was the answer. He was so kind that I thought he would be a good husband. With such a strong family upbringing he was a great catch for any girl who wanted to settle down.

"Yes! I will marry you," I answered enthusiastically, wrapping my arms around his neck in a warm embrace. And so it was that Lieutenant Jon Owen Wakely and I became engaged.

Chapter

14

ANY *GOOD* MOTHER WILL TELL YOU THAT
the love of her own child is the most powerful kind
of love on earth. So, when we finally located my
children in Albuquerque, New Mexico after not seeing them
for so long, it was truly one of the happiest moments of my
life. It was like hitting the lottery, but better.

True to his promise, Jon made every effort to help me
find my kids. Our attorney located Gus and his new wife
in Albuquerque, New Mexico. He had hidden them well
for the past two years, disappearing and ducking every
time I had been close to finding them. Even though I had
technically been given visitation rights by the judge, Gus had
disregarded those court orders and done his best to prevent
my involvement in their lives.

As we made the drive to Albuquerque, my heart was
throbbing with excitement. Jon and I played music and sang
along in the car. Our mood was a blend of anxiety, anticipation
and joy. Part of me wondered if my children had forgotten

their mother. Meanwhile, Jon was probably wondering if my kids would accept him.

Jon and I had officially tied the knot a few months ago. Since we didn't have his parents blessing, we did things quietly at the courthouse. I wore a simple satin strapless sundress. It was ivory with just a sheer sash around the waistline. Jon dressed up too, wearing his best military blues. Our ceremony was simple and private; just a celebration of us.

As we walked hand and hand from the courtroom steps, Jon picked me up and carried me to the car. Our fresh gold rings glistened in the Texas sun, representing the shining future of our new marriage.

His parents were furious when they found out, but nonetheless it was beyond their control. Jon still assured me that they would come around one day and accept me into their family, although he couldn't promise if or when. No one had been there to witness the silent unity of our wedding vows. It was just a private joining between the two of us as we became husband and wife.

More than anything, Jon gave me the stability I needed to prove to the courts that I deserved my family. It worked. Now here we were, driving up I-10 to El Paso and on to I-25 to Albuquerque. The drive took us nearly two days, which felt like two weeks as the boring scenery and cactuses whizzed by. The closer we got to New Mexico, the more excited and antsy I became.

Many thoughts ran through my head, like; "Will my children be happy to see me?" and "Will they hug me or be mad at me?" Since I hadn't even spoken to them in two years, there was no way of knowing what Gus had told them about my absence in their lives.

Finally, we arrived on the outskirts of Albuquerque. The sun set vividly across the desert mesa, making the reality of seeing Ryan and Lily again seem surreal. Technically we weren't supposed to go over to Gus's house to pick them up until the next day, due to the arrangement that was set up beforehand. However as twilight approached, both Jon and I couldn't wait to get a glimpse of their little faces so we decided to drive by their home before heading to our hotel.

As we drove down their street, my palms became sweaty with anticipation. I wasn't expecting to see the kids at that hour, especially since the sun was just going down across the Western skies of Albuquerque. But as we slowly dove down the street, we counted down the numbers on the houses. 342, 340, 338, 336, 334, 332 ... "OH, 330! There it is, Jon!" I yelled, grabbing his sleeve with excitement.

Before he had a chance to respond, I spotted little Ryan leaning up against the fence outside their home. It was a chain link fence, which gave me an unexpected opportunity to get a good look at my boy from head to toe. His nose was pressed up against the fence, as if he was expecting me. My baby boy was now four years old.

Little Ryan was holding a small hotdog on a stick. As our

car slowed on its way by, he shifted his feet in a curious way. I remember how beautiful he looked, like an angel with his sweet brown eyes still staring at the car. Everything seemed to happen in slow motion. It was like a movie reel as we made eye contact. I knew it was him. I knew it was my baby without any doubts. The last time I laid eyes on him was once in Florida a few weeks after the custody dispute in court. Not long thereafter, Gus and Susan fled with both children. It had taken so long to find them again, using every last resource I had. Plus, of course Jon helped a lot.

So now it felt like a dream, just seeing baby Ryan standing there by the fence with his little hot dog on a stick.

He didn't say a word. Neither did I. We just made eye contact as I gawked at him. When you see something you've wanted so badly finally appear before your very eyes, it is both bewildering and amazing. All I wanted to do was jump out of the car, grab my little Ryan and give him the biggest hug of his life. I longed to hold him and cuddle him and give him sweet kisses all over his chubby cheeks. But I couldn't, at least until the next day. Here he was so near, yet so far.

How unfair. After all, Ryan was my son and I gave birth to him. Who was Gus or any court system to tell me I could not hold and hug my son until tomorrow?

Tears welled up in the corners of my eyes as Jon kept on driving slowly, as he continued down the street. Little Ryan kept gazing on even after our car passed his house. I saw him in the rearview mirror, just watching intently. Maybe he felt the presence of his mother. Maybe he would be as excited to see me as I was him. A little boy never forgets his Mommy.

I barely slept at all that night. The mattress at our inexpensive motel was like lying on a hard plank, but that was not the reason I couldn't sleep. I was so nervously excited and anxious that I wanted tomorrow to come as fast as possible. I wanted to get over there as soon as the sun came up to pick up my babies. At about 8:00 a.m., we called Gus and spoke with Susan for a minute.

"We're here. We will be over to pick up the children within a half an hour," I said to her.

"That's fine. We'll have them ready," she replied.

After wolfing down a bagel and cup of coffee, I reached over and hugged Jon unexpectedly. "Thank you so much for helping me find my babies!" I told him.

"I'd do anything for you, sweetie. I love you," Jon said sincerely.

"I love you too."

We rode over to the house we had driven by the night before and this time we stopped at the end of their driveway. I wanted to run up the walkway but I skipped and then knocked on the door timidly. Gus opened it and the kids squealed on the other side. It was the first time I had seen Gus in two years. He looked pretty much the same except for some longer sideburns and a faint mustache, as if he hadn't shaven in a couple of days.

"Hey," he said. "How's it going?"

"Good, this is Jon," I replied nicely as I stepped aside for him to meet Jon.

Jon stretched out his hand politely. "How's it going? Nice to meet you."

Just then little Ryan made his appearance from around his father's waistline. "MOMMY!" he yelled, excitedly. My heart skipped a million beats as warm butterflies filled my soul with love.

As I picked him up, I gave my baby boy the biggest embrace a mom could ever muster without squishing him. My eyes lit up with unimaginable happiness as I spun him around a few times. "Mommy missed you so, so much! We're going to have so much fun together this weekend," I told him. His beaming smile warmed my heart.

Just then I spotted my daughter cautiously sitting on the edge of the couch. "Lily, Lily!" I said excitedly with arms outstretched. "Come see your Mama!"

She was a bit more shy about coming to me than Ryan was. With certain hesitation she made her way across the living room rug and put her arms around my waist. I gently reached for her little hand and said, "My how you've grown into such a beautiful little girl. I missed you, sweet angel." She looked up at me and blinked, as a small smile spread across her sweet lips. Both children were dressed nicely for my homecoming.

Susan stood in the doorway between the kitchen and

the living room. Even though I didn't know her very well, I thought her faint scowl and cool smirk indicated a look of jealousy. She didn't really say hello, she merely nodded to acknowledge Jon and I in her home. Their home. But I guess that could be expected when an "ex" spouse comes by. It was probably a little difficult for her to see me, as she sized me up in comparison. We hadn't seen each other except for once in the courtroom.

Jon and I took the kids for the entire weekend. My son was thrilled and did not leave my side, even for a second. My daughter was a little cooler but she also had a great time and warmed up to me within a couple of hours. We went to the park, the ice cream parlor, and we even took the kids to the Albuquerque State Fair. They got their faces painted. Lily chose hearts and arrows on her cheeks, while Ryan opted for the dice.

The kids really took to Jon, too. He was great with them. Jon was tall, standing at 6'2" in height. My children nicknamed him "Spider Longlegs." The name stuck throughout the years.

The whole weekend was just a big blur. It came to an end all too soon. By Monday morning I had to drop them off again with Gus and Susan. Even though they had initially looked at me like I was a stranger, they were definitely happy to see me and spend time together. Even though my daughter remembered me more than my son, little Ryan was a lot more loving towards me during that first weekend together.

"Mommy, are you going to leave us again?" my daughter

asked from the backseat of the car as we drove back to their house.

It broke my heart. "Mommy never left you, sweetie. You were taken away and I couldn't find you. I have been looking everywhere for you for the past two years," I explained to her.

However, the children had been brainwashed by my ex husband and his new wife. They were told that Mommy left them. No wonder she seemed less affectionate than I remembered. In Lily's mind I had abandoned her and little Ryan didn't really know any better since he was only four years old. Little did they know how hard I had tried to find them, spending every last resource and effort until finally we were able to see each other again. It cost me everything I owned and yet just to see them for one weekend was worth every dime I had ever earned as a grown adult.

Because Jon and I were now married, our next step was to go through the court system again to re-establish custody arrangements. We could prove that we had a solid family, which is what the judge wanted to see.

After that weekend, we saw the children every summer for two weeks, which didn't really seem long enough to establish a reconnection with them. Their family moved from New Mexico to Key West, Florida. We went on vacation every year thereafter to visit and sometimes got them during school vacations.

Jon was an angel, in a way. He took me in and cared for me at a time when I had nowhere else to turn. Without him

I would never have been able to find my children. It was unfortunate that his family did not accept me. They still didn't like me even after we were married for a couple of years because I was a "color" and because I was a few years older than he.

Every time we went there it was very unpleasant. I heard them argue sometimes and always left there crying or retreating to our room, Jon's old bedroom. His mother still had the room set up the same way he had left it, almost as if she was still hanging on to the time when he was a little boy. There were still sports memorabilia and class pictures on the wall. It seemed strange every time I was there, like staying in a little boy's room of someone who had become a man.

Jon always comforted me and told me that he loved me. He told me to be patient, that one day they would come around. I still had to refer to Jon's parents formally, being stout Baptists they were never that friendly to someone that did not fit within their mold. So I continued calling them Mr. and Mrs. Wakely for many years, although it wasn't often that I went there to visit with him.

In fact, after a few years of mistreatment I often let him go alone to visit, bowing out with some excuse to stay behind. It wasn't that they were mean to me necessarily, more like indifferent. They didn't make me feel welcome and barely said a word to me. The Wakleys just tolerated me for their son's sake because they knew it was the only way to see him.

Even though Jon was a good husband who was loyal and affectionate, he was simply not a good provider financially. The lawyer he had hired to help me find my children was based mostly on his good credit.

The reason he was not motivated to provide financial support was most likely because he had been coddled by his mother. As the apple of her eye as her only boy, Jon's mother had always taken care of him. He didn't even know how to do his own laundry and was very lazy.

Jon literally went from living with his parents to joining the military; soon thereafter meeting and marrying me. So the normal transition from boyhood to manhood never took place for him because he went from being taken care of by his mother to me. I was responsible for the both of us financially and for the upkeep of our home. The dual responsibilities of breadwinner and housewife were overwhelming.

Once again I had chosen another man who was unable to give me the lifestyle I longed for. On one hand I felt happy and grateful for his unwavering support to help me find my children. He spent a lot of time and great efforts to do this, knowing it would make me happy. And whenever they were around, my children loved him. Jon was great with them, being somewhat of a kid himself. They were able to relate.

Yet I still felt an empty hole in my heart. I gave up a lot for Jon, even drinking and other bad habits. I just wished he and I were on the same page. I still dreamed of living in a big mansion, but instead I was once again in the predicament of working two or three jobs just to keep our family alive and afloat. Meanwhile, Jon lay on the couch all day and watched sports.

The military put Jon in reserve so he lost his job. He lacked the ambition to find another job and seemed content just to have the time off. Jon was definitely a family man with a good heart, but I found it unfair having to work three jobs to provide for us while he made seemingly no effort to "man up" to the situation and go out and get some work. Just like any woman, I wanted someone to help with money and bills.

Some of my friends referred to him as the "Freeloader." After lying around the house for seven or eight months without any work, Jon finally got a job as a special Ed teacher, but it didn't pay a lot. Even worse, Jon seemed okay with it. Having a job was more to tide me over than to actually do anything that required hard work.

He was a strong Baptist and the church told Jon that "God would provide." My argument was that God would not provide for laziness.

The resentment grew on my end. How could I be this far along in my life and still poor, working in a subservient position for the government? This greatly clashed with the dreams I held on to from my childhood – of becoming a great actress, singer or someone famous. I was raised poor and still very much stuck within the lifelong rut of poverty. It was not where I longed to be, yet I could see no way to get out of it without my husband's efforts and support. He did work, but only a few hours a week. He often made excuses about there being no openings for his field. In his mind, it was enough to be married and have a life together with a wife. He had no desire for anything bigger or better. Jon was content to settle for average, at best.

It was a tough dilemma. Jon was a good supporter mentally, but not financially. He was the type of guy who would give me the last dime he had – if he had it – yet he was just not ambitious enough. I wanted someone who had high aspirations. All of my life I was a provider to others and wanted someone to finally provide for me. Was that so wrong to want? Sometimes I wondered.

Even after working two or three jobs, my responsibilities were too high within our marriage. I came home and still had to mow the lawn, clean, cook and be a good wife. He was nice to me of course, but just too lazy to do many of these tasks himself. In my mind, cutting the grass was a man's chore!

Nonetheless, my marriage and situation did not fulfill the deep yearning to be more and have more. On top of paying all of our bills, I also had to pay child support and back child support for my two children. Not to mention I had two lawyers in Florida and two in New Mexico and Texas to pay back. Our bank accounts were nearly empty because it had cost us close to $250,000 just to look for my kids. The majority of that was done based on credit. A mother would spend much more just for one day of joy with her children.

At the same time, I couldn't bring myself to leave Jon

because we had made our vows together. However, I still had a deep desire to fulfill my life's purpose or passion, whatever that may be. I wanted to "LIVE", not just exist. My search for deserved fortune was still in limbo.

After five years of patience, my feelings began to change. I still wanted to spend the rest of my life with Jon, but at the same time I had the serious longing for something bigger. There was a "something" in life I had not yet completed, although I did not yet know what it may be. Sometimes I wondered if it was just a pipedream.

Still, it was that pipedream that kept me going on the most difficult days. Time was not on my side, but I still tried to be a good wife and provider. Hence, I kept my feelings silent inside of me.

Chapter

15

THE BRIGHT NEON LIGHTS OF LAS VEGAS filled me with glee. It was like stepping into the devil's candyland. At the same time it was very romantic, with cute chapels filled with brides and grooms going out into the world for the first time as husband and wife. The colors were even more vivid than a Thomas Kinkade painting, with bright splashes of action coming from every direction.

I wanted my marriage to work, so Jon and I decided to go to Las Vegas on our seven year anniversary to renew our wedding vows. Since our first wedding had been simple at the small courthouse in Texas, I wanted something a bit more stylish and exciting for this second attempt. Somehow I felt like a renewal would make me feel secure again in our marriage. The last couple of years had been filled with resentment.

The trip was a nice reprieve from our daily routine. Working two or three jobs as the breadwinner of the household made me feel like a slave at times, especially since my duties went way beyond the normal expectations. In a way I felt obligated to Jon because of all he had done to help me find my children. There were also those internal feelings of guilt over getting divorced a second time. After all, my mother had stuck it out until the very end with my father and he had not been an ideal husband in return. Maybe it was just what I was used to, but at times I couldn't help feeling remorseful for the decision to dive into the relationship with Jon without living together first.

He was a good man and never cheated or treated me badly. It was just his laziness and lack of fiscal responsibility that mainly drove me nuts. Before we went to Las Vegas to renew our vows, Jon and I had discussed this to great lengths. I told him that I needed more and he promised to fulfill my needs.

Jon was the one in our relationship who had a higher education, so he should have been the one providing for me. I had very little to no education beyond the GED that I had earned during my marriage to Gus. Yet I was the determined one. He was not. To me, this proved a point that it is not necessary to have a higher education in order to be successful in life. All you truly need is drive and ambition. You have to want success; it doesn't just fall in your lap while you're sitting on your duff in front of the TV.

Jon also left me frequently to go visit his family in Mississippi. I felt neglected whenever he left. He began going to visit them without me because even though we had been married for many years, his parents still never accepted me. Of course I didn't enjoy going over there, either. Why waste time and effort getting to know people who don't want to know you anyway?

Even though the trip to Vegas was supposed to rejuvenate our marriage and give us new hope, Jon's hobbies and interests always came first. I continued taking care of him just like his mother had. Perhaps that was the reason he had chosen to marry a woman who was eleven years older than he was. Besides working two or three jobs, I was responsible for cleaning the entire house, cutting the grass, cooking, doing dishes, washing and folding our laundry, as well as many other chores which should have been shared duties.

Plain and simple, Jon was lazy. His passions were baseball, football and basketball. Basically, he loved sports on TV during every season. Too many, as far as I was concerned. Having someone else to manage the workload for him, Jon didn't have any inkling whatsoever – not one iota – about common knowledge self-management skills. He couldn't even write a check, clean, pay bills (much less have any concept of bill-paying), cook or do anything for himself. Jon was helpless. This is something I never would have suspected when I met him and realized he had achieved a bachelor's degree. How could someone who had managed to graduate college become so helpless?

One day as he was watching another boring baseball game I blurted out, "I'm going to go get a shovel and get this couch up before the roots grow underneath it."

He didn't really respond, just looked at me funny. So I went out to the shed and brought in a shovel, tossing it right next to him.

I knew Jon cared for me and probably loved me, but our major marital difference was in the critical lack of ambition on his part; whereas I had more drive than a team of oxen pulling a wagon to the moon. It didn't even faze him. Jon was perfectly content with what we had, not realizing that if we both worked together we could have accomplished so much more in a shorter amount of time. However, Jon's philosophy was that as long as he had a roof over his head and food on the table, then he was happy. Those two things alone were more than enough to please him in life.

So after we returned from our wedding renewal in Las Vegas, we both felt rejuvenated in the relationship. Jon finally got a job teaching, but we still had a mound of debt that looked like an insurmountable Himalaya.

Not long thereafter, I started feeling very sick. The doctors diagnosed me with uterine cancer that was treatable, yet it still nearly cost me my life. The cancer chemotherapy caused severe nausea, vomiting and soreness, as well as fatigue and pain. For several weeks I laid in a hospital bed with sweat pouring down my forehead and behind my neck.

Fading in and out of consciousness, I often slept as my body tried to heal. Thank goodness I had health insurance through my job with the military, otherwise that would have been one more deadly bill to add to our growing pile. During

161

that few weeks off when I was not working, it only contributed to our huge pile of repayments.

Jon was there for me the whole time. He held my hand throughout all of the procedures, even while I was unconscious. It was finally his chance to take care of me, but in a different way than I had done for him for the past seven years. He was there for me.

I did recover in due time, at least enough to go to work again. Although I wasn't 100% my old self I was strong inside mentally. After making it this far in life and yearning for more, I knew it wasn't my time yet to die. Especially after the lesson I had learned from the accident in the cemetery. That wake-up call had been enough for me to appreciate living. Plus I didn't want to let my kids down, even though I didn't get a chance to see them often. We spoke on the phone a lot as they grew older and more curious about their mother.

It was after my recovery that I came to the realization that Jon did not have the same goals in life as I did. He was the type to settle and would always be okay with averageness. The promises he made before we renewed our vows in Las Vegas had already been forgotten because they were made with the intent of appeasing me, not sincerity.

My feelings started going in a different direction, one that was pulling me away from the relationship. I wanted to move forward and do more with my life, rather than being a slave to a helpless man. Jon and I were married in 1990. It was eight or nine years after our marriage that I began giving up on

Jon and the hope that he might ever do something useful and productive. Sadly, he just didn't have it in him. No amount of encouragement or prodding could force him, either.

We had other problems, too. Jon's startling jealous side came out when I tried to expand my social circle and go hang out with friends. I was no longer content with going home early every night, knowing that my life revolved around the dirty laundry and stacks of dishes waiting for me there. So instead, I decided to go out and have fun. It made me happier inside to have like-minded friends and social circles. My naturally gregarious nature needed stimulation that Jon could not, or refused to provide. His droning baseball and football shows were not enough to make me happy. TV just wasn't my thing.

Sometimes I even invited him out, but Jon declined to go. He didn't like to go out any more than I liked to stay in and be bored at home. At the same time, he didn't want me to go either.

I always wanted to walk forward, not backward. My philosophy has always been; "Going forward is the only way to get ahead; going behind does nothing." So I didn't want to just sit idly on the couch and let life pass me by. With a naturally energetic spirit and a deep burning urge to succeed, it was clear that Jon was only hindering my ability to move forward. I didn't want anyone to stand in my way.

Ideally, I just wanted Jon to be on the same page as I was and to get his butt up off the couch and go do something worthwhile with that great education he had. He did not have the entrepreneurial mindset. In fact, during the time we were married I think he had at least eight or nine different jobs. He couldn't stick to the same thing because he was unstable and lacked the drive to get promoted or to make any moves towards managerial positions. For Jon, the bottom of the totem pole was just enough to appease me.

Once I finally came to this realization and began doing more for myself, it was liberating. I felt like I had one of those "Get Out of Jail Free" cards from a Monopoly game. After this epiphany, good things began. It proved to be a point that people should follow their own pursuits in life and never let anyone hold them back from chasing their own dreams.

"Either get on board and come with me, or get off the train and do your own thing," I told Jon one day. This was my attitude towards our marriage.

I transferred jobs from San Angelo to San Antonio, despite Jon's attempts to keep me locked up at home like a prisoner. I told him it would be a better life for us. Still unable to bring myself to leave him altogether, I brought him along for the move.

My new job opportunity was at a hospital for the military as a facility manager assistant. It was similar to the front desk job at the stationary housing, yet it was a different atmosphere for me to work in a fast-paced hospital as opposed to the more laid back surroundings of a hotel.

It was at this job that I met a lady named Anna who also

worked at the hospital as a pharmaceutical primary care facilitator. Within a few weeks we became fast friends. She too, was from Thailand.

That was not the only thing that Anna and I had in common. Like me, Anna was ambitious. She was raised as a business-oriented, catholic girl. Every day we took lunch at the same time and sat together at the hospital cafeteria. She talked about how to invest money and gave me great ideas. Starstruck, I took in every word. Why had I not met Anna sooner? Maybe she was the answer I had been searching for. Instead of relying on men to help me find wealth, I soon realized that the only person worth relying on – EVER – in life is me.

Anna enjoyed my sense of humor. "You a funny lady," she told me often, with her charming Thai accent. We laughed and frequently went out on the town in the evenings. I had someone to hang out with that was just like me in many ways.

One afternoon as I was biting into the cardboard tuna sandwich from the hospital cafeteria, Anna said; "Hey, let's venture out and do some investing together." Every day she talked about how to invest money and how hot the real estate market was at that time. In fact, Anna had purchased two houses that were now being rented out. Real estate had proven to be very lucrative for her thus far.

Skeptical, yet naturally curious, I asked Anna many questions about investing. My credit was ruined by the divorce and debt to search for my children, so I wondered just how someone like me could ever make money in the real estate business. Anna explained how she worked with an investor who fronted the money and acted as a silent partner, while she did most of the legwork. The investor actually bought the homes and financed the investment. This was when I first learned about "flipping" homes. It was intriguing.

I was interested and figured I had nothing to lose. After all, my whole life had been spent chasing a dream, so now when finally faced with an opportunity to react, I knew I had to seize my chance. Hence, Anna introduced me to the investor she had been working with. They even bought my house in San Angelo to show me how to do it.

However, I still didn't have my first deal quite yet. More than a little wet behind the ears and definitely outside of my zone of comfort, it took an extra nudge to finally give me the extra confidence I needed.

Like so many other people in the world who settle or who don't know any better, my only knowledge of earning money was to toil away for peanut minimum wages, which I had done for the majority of my adulthood. Having never been an entrepreneur before, the idea of becoming an investor seemed outlandishness and surreal. By the same token, I was curious and just daring enough to do it. 'Why not me? If these people can become rich in real estate, so can I!'

Anna gave me the confidence to do it by setting a good example of her success. That was how I finally embraced the entrepreneurial mindset, rather than trying to think of other ways to find wealth. Marrying a military man had certainly not been the answer. Not twice. My only ticket to wealth was to take matters into my own hands. I put aside my misconception that only college educated people can be successful with investing. In reality, anybody with enough ambition can be successful.

One thing was certain. I was looking for a more stable life. A life I didn't have to be a slave to the system, nor to any man. Finally, I felt like my long sought-after dreams of living in a fancy mansion one day were just around the bend. In fact, those dreams were closer and more real than ever.

All I needed was to find a partner, someone who believed in me and who was on the same page. That was how I met Henry.

Henry was a hospital administrator through the Air Force. He was in the military a few years, still serving active duty. At age 25, Henry was extremely intelligent and ambitious. In fact, he went into the Air Force as a Captain and soon thereafter he earned his master's degree.

We were already friends through work so we often talked about fascinating topics. Henry was also a teacher and received many accolades in academics. I admired his 'smarts' and I think he enjoyed my sense of humor.

Ironically, one of Henry's students brought a box to him one day that he had purchased at a yard sale. Within its contents was an entire real estate program that someone had bought from the Carleton Sheets infomercial and never used.

It's probably rare to hear anyone say that an infomercial changed their life. Most people watch them for about three minutes out of curiosity and then switch to another channel. But obviously someone watches them and buys the products advertised on them. Otherwise, infomercials would not still be a popular sales tool.

When Henry first told me about it, we had already been discussing the idea of investing in real estate together. He told me about the box that had been given to him and that he found the information to be exciting.

Still not entirely "savvy" with the English language, I misheard the name he mentioned as the narrator. "Cotton Sheets? Who the heck is Cotton Sheets?" I asked him.

"NO!" Henry said, laughing. "Car-le-ton Sheets. With an 'R'. Not cotton. I swear Nancy, you really make me laugh."

"Well, what is it?" I asked.

"I'll have to show you," he replied. "I can't really explain it but it's like a big kit that has tools and tricks of the trade to buy beat-up homes and fix them up and flip them quick for a profit."

The first time, we watched the 'Cotton Sheets' program together. I learned a lot of the tricks of the trade. There was a book and some tools to figure out how much the real estate was worth. I read the book several times and even showed it to Anna.

Anna inspired and encouraged me to be successful. Both she and Henry empowered me with the knowledge. Carleton

THE QUEST FOR SERENDIPITY

Sheets was the most informational resource I had, but I was so absorbed and eager that I began reading other books like the Millionaire Next Door, Millionaire Minds and other millionaire mentality books. My favorites were some of the books written by Donald Trump. Reading all of these books gave me immense confidence. I got smart and learned the tricks to become successful.

Subsequently, Henry became my business partner. Once we had established trust and friendship, I proposed that we buy a house using his credit and with my partnership. He was just as enthused about making money as I was. At 25, he was brilliant about many things already, including management of finances. This was the polar opposite of my husband, who had no ambition and no knowledge of finances whatsoever.

Making new friends outside of my marriage was just what I needed to build my self-esteem and put me on the right track towards fulfilling my lifelong dreams. It was liberating and fun to have a new hobby that was positive and stimulating.

Henry and I scoured the newspaper and other sources. Looking for our first investment property was exciting and we didn't want to make the wrong choice. With his meticulous nature and my natural sense for business, Henry and I finally spotted a gem.

It was a foreclosure property; a little brick bungalow in a nice neighborhood of San Antonio. Although it needed work because of the former property owners allowing it to become run down, we both saw the potential in it. Using some of our learned skills, we calculated how much it would cost o fix it up and resell it. Our intent was to "flip" it as quickly as possible so that we could move on to the next house and the next one after that.

We submitted an offer to the bank and it was accepted. Scary as it seemed, we had officially made our first investment and felt good about it. The very same day we bought it, Henry and I went over to assess the damages and begin the process of rejuvenation.

We ripped up the soiled carpets and had hardwood floors installed throughout the rooms. We painted and hired a landscaping company to come over and fix up the yard, which had become a field of overgrown dandelions and weeds. For two solid weeks we worked diligently until finally we were both happy with the outcome. The charming brick bungalow finally had beauty and desirability once again. It cost us approximately $8,300 to spruce up the house and make it look new again. Doing some of the work ourselves helped us shave the costs of hiring laborers.

As we stood back in admiration of our first investment, Henry and I were very proud. I was pleased to have his friendship and grateful for his inspiration and guidance. He was not just my business partner, he was a new great friend who inspired me to better myself and encouraged me to pursue my dreams. My life changed from the darkness of knowing struggle to the brightness of hope and promise.

A real estate broker we met through Anna came over the

next day. She brought an appraiser over the same afternoon and by the following day we learned that all of our work had paid off. The home was now worth $60,000 more than we had paid for it. And the market was hot. People were looking for these family style homes in great neighborhoods, just like the house we had bought and fixed to flip for a quick sale.

It worked. Within three weeks we had three offers on the table. Henry and I chose the one that would yield the most profit. The sale was quick and the $44,000 profit made us jump for joy. Now we had even more ammunition and ambition to continue our new adventures in real estate investing!

Chapter

16

"I'LL TAKE THE SILVER ONE," I SAID TO THE smiling salesman with the yellow hair and skinny mustache. His red suspenders stood out under his suit like someone trying to hide a bright red candy apple underneath a white handkerchief.

"Very nice choice, Mrs. Wakely. Do you want me to direct you to the finance department?" he asked, eagerly.

"That won't be necessary. I'll be paying cash." I told him.

"Cash?" he looked surprised, yet pleased. "Um, okay. Well let's go inside and go over the details."

I followed him inside the spacious and clean car dealership. Hungry salesmen were lined up like wolves swirling around a little fawn. Their fake smiles and cordial hellos were actually pangs of jealousy over the fact that I had already been taken as a customer by the yellow-haired salesman. That's how salesmen are. They're never truly happy when someone else on the team makes a sale.

Nevertheless, I was excited. No one could wipe the smile off my face, not even with a whole bottle of Windex. Today

THE QUEST FOR SERENDIPITY

I was buying my first brand new car; a shiny silver BMW. It was my dream car and to me this vehicle represented just one of the many goals I had accomplished. I was finally going up!

In the past I had always purchased cars by either scouring through classified ads or having one of my friends tell me about a "deal" on a used car they had spotted on the way to work.

My soon-to-be 'MINE' silver BMW was a real milestone of wealth, one I had dreamed of and prayed for. It was finally my turn and I had finally overcome the lifetime of poverty.

Henry and I had continued with our wealth building through the real estate market. We made a great team. I was good at locating the properties and doing a lot of the legwork, while he was great with numbers and figuring out how much we could anticipate and if the deal was worth it in the end. Almost every time, he had been right on the money ... literally.

We continued buying houses and spent some money fixing them up. We were careful to choose easy fixes, none that needed complete overhauls. Most of the remodeling or revamping the homes needed was only cosmetic or electrical and roofing updates. Floors, paint, landscaping or even knocking down a wall here or there were things we did to improve the homes enough to flip them. Nearly all of them were foreclosures and we followed the 'Cotton Sheets' program very well.

By the time I was finally able to buy my dream car, we had already done fifteen houses and even a couple of commercial properties. Even though I treated myself to a lot of the luxuries I had never been able to afford before, it was also a great sigh of relief to finally tackle the massive debt that had built up from years of searching for my children. I paid off the lawyers, the collection agencies, and everything. The money leftover was mine. And I truly enjoyed and deserved it!

Flipping houses with Henry was fun. We got to know the ins and outs of the industry and overcame our mistakes easily. We became very good at it. We were real estate experts.

I was also very grateful to Henry. Without his guidance and financial backing I would never have been able to get rich. We split everything evenly. 50 / 50. For the first time in my life I was able to splurge and buy things that I had only dreamed of when I was poor, homeless or struggling just to live.

However, I also knew the importance of giving back. I sponsored organizations that I wanted to be in when I was young. I helped my family and was often giving and providing to other people, which made me feel really good inside. Better than a basketful of kittens.

Meanwhile, Jon got a new job that required us to move to the Florida panhandle. It was at the Eglin Air Force Base, just shy of Valparaiso, Florida near the middle of the Gulf of Mexico. The timing was not so good for me, but Jon was happy to be closer to his family. He was also very happy with the gravy train of money and felt entitled to my newfound wealth. Therefore, he was not willing to let me go.

I threatened to end things several times, since he did not contribute to our relationship – neither financially nor by doing any housework. But it was more than that. I had lost my luster for Jon. He just didn't try and lacked the drive to pursue any passion in life. His complacency was the disconnector of our marriage. Yet now that I was making money in real estate Jon was more determined than ever to keep me around. It was his ticket to laziness. The transfer to Eglin AFB was just a job to placate my nagging about getting a job. So, he was able to get away with doing very little but living very large in return. Jon was a true freeloader who depended on women his whole life to take care of him.

When he moved it would have been another chance to leave him, except for some reason I still could not bring myself to do it. Maybe I was scared. Even though he seemed too lazy to do so, while Jon served in the military he was involved in military intelligence and the secret service. That was how he had been able to find my children for me so many moons ago, using his military connections in conjunction with racking up our debt with good attorneys. So, every time I threatened to leave him, Jon said he would hunt me down. Even though he had never shown any signs of physical abuse, I was still kind of afraid of what he might do if he found me.

The other problem with leaving Jon was the stability he

still offered. My children finally came to live with me after I became wealthy. I wanted to have them with me all along, but even as they grew older they had chosen to stay with their father. Money has a way of affecting people, even children. Finally having a chance to spoil them was nice, but raising teenagers is a very difficult task in itself, especially when your children haven't formed the bond that typically occurs between mother and child. Even though I had no control over that fact, they were still my kids and I wanted them to be with me. It was something I always wanted all along but never got the chance to experience, so I hoped that having them move in with me would give us the chance to reconnect.

My kids always liked Jon. He was always there, like a faithful dog that always waits for you to come home. Meanwhile, I was still doing investments in Texas. Even though my hospital job retired me early, I still kept my foot in the door to maintain my benefits. I didn't mind that they retired my position sooner than planned because it gave me even more time to spend on real estate investing with Henry.

The only way I could make it work to continue the real estate investments while living in Florida was to drive to San Antonio every two weeks. Jon stayed behind with my kids. Ryan was still in middle school and Lily was almost ready to graduate. Nevertheless, I was able to spend more time with them than ever before and make up for many years of lost time, even though I was gone a lot for my job.

THE QUEST FOR SERENDIPITY

My bank account started getting bigger and bigger. My dreams started coming true. I was even in a position to loan money as an investor for others who had ideas they wanted to get off the ground, which brought in even more profits once they repaid. It was like being a loan shark, much like the guys who had loaned money to my father that he had been unable to repay. The difference was that I did not loan money to people for frivolous ventures.

Occasionally I made a few bad decisions and learned a few lessons with regards to people's character. Whenever you have money, people come to you with palms outstretched. Needy chicklings try to take advantage of people with money. One guy that I loaned money to even had an airplane as collateral. So, Henry and I became the proud owners of our very own airplane.

We also acquired some commercial properties as we got better and better at flipping real estate. One deal we landed upon was for a Holiday Inn that we purchased for $750,000 and then turned around and sold for $900,000. We also purchased a Quality Inn. In my wildest dreams never would have imagined being the owner of a hotel and an airplane!

Life was good except for my marriage. The intimacy between Jon and I had been gone for so long I could barely remember what it was like to begin with. He spent my money on things he always wanted to do. Being a huge sports fanatic, he often flew to Miami for the Dolphins games during football season. He became lazier than ever after I hired a housekeeper to keep up with all of the chores I could no longer attend to.

After we became better acquainted, my housekeeper Ida said to me one day, "Your husband is lazy! You live in a big house and have a great career, but all he does is work for a few hours a week on the base. The rest of the time he just sits on the couch and watches TV."

"I know, Ida. I am sure you must be sick of picking up after a grown man, as I was for so many years," I agreed.

When brought to my attention by an outsider, my husband's lack of effort made me even more upset. I still wanted to cut ties with him, but decided to wait until after the kids graduated high school. It was needless to upset them at this point, especially after missing out on much of their childhood.

The teenage years were very difficult though. My son refused to listen to me and did not respect me. I caught him smoking pot a few times and even carrying it to school. Throughout their childhood, my kids had come to believe that their mother left them. Quite the opposite was true. Gus took them away and I had no choice in the matter. I spent every last dime and most of my time trying to locate them, but they were much too young to remember. Instead, my ex and his wife brainwashed them to believe I did not care.

The kids both had fierce tempers. They must have learned these characteristics from my ex-husband. During one argument my son struck me across the face so I had to call the police and have him put in jail for a night. Since he was a minor it did not affect his record, but it certainly was a wakeup call to him. Ryan needed to learn respect for women, especially towards his mother. That was something his father never taught him because he didn't know how to do it himself.

It was difficult to throw my own son in jail, yet something I had to do to teach him a lesson. Obviously he must have witnessed his father striking Susan at some point during his childhood, because abuse was a learned behavior. He sharpened up after that incident and never hit me again.

My daughter came with her own set of problems. She was unruly and spiteful towards me in every way. Lily was older when Gus took the kids so she really took it to heart. She was always cold to me ever since the day they went to live with their Dad. She was tough to get close to. To this day I still long for the bond with her that I missed out on much like the bond I shared with my own mother who I was so very close to.

Lily showed signs of drug abuse, although she firmly denied doing any drugs except marijuana. Even though I was naïve about drugs and the common types kids were using these days, I definitely noticed signs in her behavior that were very different than someone who stays clean.

To top it off, when she was seventeen Lily informed me that she was pregnant. She had been sneaking out with some kid named 'Teddy-T', who had piercings and tattoos. Teddy-T was just another local badass looking to get a piece of tail and have some fun, but my daughter was not wise to the ways of young males in the world. He was an older kid of about nineteen and had a big chip on his shoulder.

I knew they were doing drugs together, although I couldn't determine what kind. Their red eyes, angry behaviors and irrational decisions said it all. Once Teddy-T found out that Lily was pregnant, it was no surprise that he went running in the other direction. He did not want to be a father; he was just a teenager who wanted to have fun, do drugs and get laid. Becoming a Dad was not in his nature so he bolted.

The news made me angry. I did not want her to have a baby that was deformed or messed up because of drugs. Even without Teddy-T, I think she was still addicted and doing drugs, despite the news of pregnancy. As to be expected, Lily denied her drug use and it became a huge argument between us.

Even though it went against my principles, I encouraged Lily to have an abortion. After all, she was only seventeen at the time. Having a drug-addicted or deformed baby was not the outcome I wanted for her in life. She didn't know the first thing about motherhood and I felt that she wasn't ready. What if she abandoned or abused her child? That was something drug addicts often do.

Jon and I were not in agreement on the topic, which only stirred the anger within our household. Our relationship became worse than ever because Jon was a firm Baptist who did not believe in abortion, no matter what the circumstances.

THE QUEST FOR SERENDIPITY

The controversy between pro-choice and pro-life became very real for me because of my daughter's irresponsibility.

Deep down, I knew that she was unprepared to be a mother and that she would not take care of a baby. Her swollen eyes and beads of sweat gave away her secrets of addiction. The child would have been left for someone else to raise and would have been brought into a world of anger, instead of love. Thinking about my first grandbaby as a deformed or addicted newborn was grotesque. The baby would have been alone and abandoned. These qualities mess children up when they are young and cause many problems as they grow into adults. That is, if she were to have had the baby.

She hated me for it but I took Lily to get a drug test. The results came back positive, which infuriated me. I decided the only option was to end the pregnancy so I took her to a private clinic. This powerful move severed the possibility of having any kind of connection with my daughter at that point in our lives. She was so upset and mad about it that she chose to go back to Key West to live with her father.

Fortunately, her life turned out just fine because she cleaned up her act and stopped doing drugs altogether. She met her future husband, Will and they went on to have a beautiful child together. Despite her hatred and resentment of me, I continued providing for her and always gave Lily a place to live, clothes, money, and everything she needed. None of these material things were appreciated but to this day they are still expected.

Having a lot of money had its unexpected drawbacks. The lack of appreciation was definitely the biggest one. The less advantaged members of the family relied on the one who served as the provider, leaving the entire burden on the main earner. Namely, me.

Eventually my daughter came around after a few years of pacification and forgiveness. She gave up drugs and began attending church. When she returned to our home a few years later, she brought Will and the baby with her. I wanted them to have their own place, so of course I helped to provide them with one. Lily, Jon and Will began going to Jon's church with him every Sunday. They became Baptists.

I gave Lily enough money to take care of everything for her and her whole family. She finally finished college seven years after enrolling, but motherhood and her husband were always Lily's main priorities. My son-in-law also went to school to become a computer technician.

I often helped him, too. I opened a store for him to work at so that he could earn money. I didn't want him to become a freeloader like my husband Jon was. Unfortunately, he also lacked the ambition and after a brief spell of working there, Will didn't want to do it anymore. Just like everyone else in my family, his attitude was; "Well, my mother-in-law will provide for me." All of them adopted the same philosophy as Jon, assuming that I would just give them money anytime they needed it. They all became spoiled and content with letting me do so.

"Don't worry, God will provide," was Jon's attitude whenever I asked him to help me more or to push him to help me financially.

My son, daughter and son-in-law all adopted the same philosophy. On one hand I wanted to help them because it was in my generous nature to do so. After all, I loved them and felt like with money and material gifts I could show them how much. On the other hand, I felt taken for granted, underappreciated and a lack of gratitude all around me.

I began wanting to escape them all. At least, paying their way. They needed to learn how to fend for themselves and the only way to learn was through my absence. It was finally time to do for Nancy and to let others learn how to take care of their lives without me, at least for now.

I wanted to wake up one morning and have one store that I could enjoy working at while I was investing in real estate with Henry. And most of all, I didn't want to owe anybody anything or take care of anybody except me. There were times I questioned their love for me because every day they all just wanted me to give, give, give ... but none of them knew how to give back. The most appreciation I ever received was a "Thanks, you're the best," delivered with a tone of insincerity.

The giving of money and material things became less enjoyable and mostly expected. Subsequently, my longing to escape my marriage, my family and my life of being taken advantage of became a burning desire that I could no longer ignore. Plus the bills were piling up again, even though

I was making great money. People had their hands out in every direction, leading to more money going out than what was coming in. Providing for everyone was bleeding me dry financially.

None of my children followed my example of success. Even though I loved them very much, I felt that it was time to cut the cords. And with Jon, I felt as though my life had become his and that years of unhappiness had taken its toll on my soul.

So I prepared to leave, getting everything ready. I decided to be somewhat sneaky because I knew they would all be upset at first. Cutting off their endless financial crutch was going to be difficult for everyone. Yet it was something I had to do in order to maintain my self-respect.

That was the plan.

But the day I was prepared to leave, I got one phone call from Seattle that would change my whole life and all of my imminent plans. It was my sister's friend, Layla.

"I'm sorry to be the bearer of bad news, Nancy."

"What is it Layla?" I asked, hesitantly.

"It's Penny. Your sister. She's been murdered."

Chapter
17

WHAT BECAME OF MY SISTER'S FATE started back when I was married to Gus and we all moved back to the United States from the Philippines. After someone stole Penny's Visa it was of great disappointment for me, my mom and especially for Penny. We were all very close.

We were never able to satisfy the paperwork and get a new Visa for her, so my sister was deported back to Thailand. Even though we still tried to get her to the U.S., it was unfortunately the same time that Gus ran off to Colorado and then my Mother became very ill with cancer. Since I was working three jobs, taking care of my children and my mother, I simply had no money left to try to fight the legal battle that was necessary to retrieve my sister. I sometimes wonder if Penny's life would have turned out differently had she come to the U.S. with us back then.

Instead, Penny was in Thailand to stay. After she saw our Mom through her final days of cancer, Penny met a man named Mike. Mike was in the Navy and was stationed at

Nakhon Phanom Royal Thai Navy Base along the Mekong River. It was once an Air Force base and front line of the insurgency for the United States during the Vietnam War until 1975, when the war finally ended. Perhaps following in the footsteps of her big sister, Penny saw her marriage to Mike as a ticket to the U.S. They moved to Seattle, Washington and made a life there.

Although I didn't get to see her very often, we spoke on the phone and wrote letters. Penny came to visit not long after moving to America. We always remained close and she was the only sibling that I ever really knew or had any kind of connection with.

We spoke at least a couple of times each month. Mike was then deployed to the Pearl Harbor Naval Station in Honolulu, Hawaii. Of course Penny was right by his side as they transferred even further away. At least in Hawaii she was still on U.S. soil.

Like me, Penny was a hard worker and found a job in Honolulu working at a medical clinic. She made a few friends but she was more introverted than I was. For the most part, Penny was a peaceful person with a big heart. She did not aspire to be famous but was not willing to settle for unhappiness.

That is why I was not surprised when she divorced Mike not long after they moved to Hawaii. Over time I noticed her growing discontent with his actions. Like our father and my ex-husband Gus, Mike also liked the bottle. Frequently he was spotted with his sidekick, Jack Daniels or with his co-workers at the local bar. Hawaii is known for its Tiki Huts and colorful beverages. Apparently Mike had a problem saying no to the temptations of alcohol. This made my sister very unhappy. She wanted things to work out with him and genuinely loved Mike, but she just couldn't live with the unstable personality of an alcoholic.

I met Mike once and thought he was super nice. He was polite and handsome. But I couldn't blame my sister for being unhappy with the drinking. It was something we grew up with and were familiar with because of our father; however it was a problem that only brought on even more marital dysfunction.

Instead of having a family with Mike, Penny divorced him after her green card and citizenship were solid. Even though it may have seemed harsh, it was accepted under the circumstances.

The decision partially had something to do with a newfound friendship she made with a man named Tommy Songlee. Although Tommy was not in the military, he was definitely a man of uniform. Having worked for Northwest Airlines for well over a decade, Tommy's charming and suave persona pulled her in like a Venus flytrap.

The two had a lot in common. Tommy's parents lived in Seattle, which was the only place within the States that my sister knew and felt comfortable. His real mother was also from Thailand, so he had been there a lot growing up and was familiar with the customs. Even though his father and stepmother raised him, he had been in close contact with his birth mother. Tommy went to visit her every summer. He came to love the country and it was a topic he and my sister often spoke about throughout their courtship.

Most of all, Tommy offered stability. His long career with the airlines meant that he was able to hold a prestigious job, earn money and provide Penny with the type of lifestyle she longed for. Being a pilot also meant that he was not a drinker, otherwise he would not have been able to hold his position there for so long. This was another aspect of his personality that appealed to her. In Penny's eyes, Tommy was 'the one' who she could have a family with.

She fell hard and fast for him. I'll never forget the happiness in her voice, which was much different than it had been with Mike. She swooned like a beautiful swan that had been plucked from a lake. What she didn't know was that the love of her life was actually a devious hungry wolf that had been sitting on the shore the whole time, just waiting for an innocent swan to swim by so he could make his move.

Penny and Tommy were married just a few months after their whirlwind romance. He was everything she longed for and she was on cloud eleven, just a couple of steps above nine. They moved to Seattle to be closer to his family. Penny got along well with them and she became very friendly with Tommy's stepmother.

For the first five or six years of their marriage, they seemed very happy. She spoke very highly of him and although he frequently traveled as a pilot, my sister was accepting of it because Tommy was a good provider. She didn't really have to work, although she did go to adult Ed classes to hone in on her English skills. She also took a few hobby types of classes and worked part-time just to have something to do on the days Tommy was away.

It wasn't until they decided to have a child that Tommy's behavior changed drastically. My sister longed for a child and a family so the couple had been trying to conceive for a couple of years. Finally, she called me with the exciting news. "I'm pregnant!"

"That's great, Penny. I'm so happy for you!" I said, overjoyed. I knew she wanted a baby of her own to love and care for. Penny's biological clock was not just ticking, by then it ticked louder than a metronome.

"Yes, and Tommy's mother is moving here from Thailand to come live with us," explained my sister. "She will be a big help with the baby."

"I'm happy to hear that. You need all the help you can get," I said with sisterly pride.

Penny said, "I think we need a bigger place. Tommy is buying us a house in Tacoma."

"Oh really? You deserve it, dear sister," I offered my words of encouragement. It was nice to hear her joyful tone through the receiver.

They did buy a house in Tacoma. It was a light blue ranch style home with an upstairs loft and four bedrooms, which offered plenty of room both for Tommy's mother to come live with them and for their soon-to-be new arrival, Penny's baby boy.

After Penny gave him a son, Tommy changed a lot. He became controlling. He ordered her around. And part of the problem was my sister's mother-in-law. She had never lived in the United States but it was clear that she was very jealous of the relationship between her son and his wife.

Even though she was not the one to raise Tommy, she was not happy about the fact that Penny was friendly with Tommy's stepmother. It was worse than the evil stepmother you read about in fairy tales and Penny was very upset by her presence. All she wanted was to raise her newborn baby in peace and to enjoy her family. But Tommy's mother poisoned his mind to the point of evident fury.

From Tommy's perspective, he finally had the relationship with his real mother he had wanted throughout his whole life, just as every little boy who loves his mother does. He wanted so badly to believe the things she said. Sometimes Tommy's mother accused Penny of cheating while he was away on a layover with the airlines. His mind became enraged, which resulted in fights between him and my sister. Even though she denied it and pointed the finger back to his mother, Tommy would not believe her.

"She's coming between us! You need to have her move out!" my sister pleaded. Ultimately, her intrusion led to the first incidents of physical abuse.

THE QUEST FOR SERENDIPITY

In addition to the name calling, Tommy punched Penny in the face on more than one occasion. He believed wholeheartedly that she was cheating on him, when in fact she was home raising their son, running errands, going to school or working. Penny loved him and was not the type to be unfaithful to her husband.

While he was away, Penny had his mother to deal with. They fought daily and her mother-in-law even invited a bunch of unwanted guests from Thailand to their home. Interns, exchange students and friends were invited for days, weeks or even a couple of months. This really pissed Penny off. It was her home, and how dare Tommy's evil mother defy her private space? She ordered some of the guests to leave and insisted behind closed doors that Tommy banish her from their home.

It was clear that Penny's mother-in-law had one goal in mind – and that was to drive Penny out of her son's life. This bizarre quest for selfishness and family turmoil changed Tommy in many ways, both personally and professionally. He started missing work and getting into trouble. After working for Northwest for nearly twenty years, Tommy became unreliable and was on the verge of getting fired. He was stretched out beyond his limit of understanding, like a rubber band that was about to snap.

By the time their son entered school, little Alec had already witnessed the horrors of his parents' marriage. At only five years old, my poor nephew had seen his mother mistreated by his father on many occasions. Alec drowned his troubles at home by playing baseball and developed a strong passion for the game. Alec lived, breathed and absorbed himself in everything baseball. Baseball cards, baseball playing, baseball watching and baseball comic books. He tuned out the fighting with baseball.

Tommy's personality grew more bizarre with each passing week. He stopped coming home when he was supposed to and after all of the accusations he had made with regards to Penny cheating it turned out he had a mistress of his own. This revelation on behalf of my sister brought about even more drama.

Tommy's mistress was a flight attendant. She was someone that he had worked with on many of his trips. Since he was employed by the airlines for many years, Tommy had established some seniority over the other less experienced pilots. He was able to pick and choose the trips he wanted to take. Some of his favorites were the easy flights to New York or Boston from Seattle. However, after he hooked up with the flight attendant he began taking more layovers. Well, at least that was what he told his family.

Honestly, Penny was happier when he was gone. Instead of tiptoeing around him and wondering if he was going to beat the shit out of her, she was able to relax more when Tommy was gone. She plotted her escape and worried more and more every time the abuse escalated. He continued his accusations of cheating. It was the pot calling the kettle black.

THE QUEST FOR SERENDIPITY

After missing enough work due to all of the problems at home, Northwest fired Tommy from his job he held for over twenty years. Devastated, he developed an enraged anger that affected his face and even the way he looked. The negative aura that exuded from his whole body was something that could not be overlooked, even by strangers. It was like the devil had entered his soul as he lived life much like a mysterious minefield that no one dared or hoped to step on one day for fear that it might explode.

Losing his job made Tommy crazy. A bezerk kind of crazy, from a mental standpoint. We weren't sure if he still had the mistress or not, but some days he disappeared for hours and came back with a fury that his family feared. Tommy tricked my sister and his mother into selling their house in Tacoma, claiming it was time to move to Las Vegas and begin a whole new life with a fresh start.

Surprisingly, the house sold quickly. Not so surprisingly, Tommy's intent was not to move the whole family to Las Vegas. Instead, he kidnapped little Alec and took him to Las Vegas on his own. My sister was distraught over her missing son. She had been planning to move, but not with Tommy. Penny was stashing away all of her money, just waiting for the right time to escape with her little boy and come live with me in Florida.

When she showed up on my doorstep without her son and with years' worth of bruises, I was shocked at how different Penny looked. She was still my sister but she was pale, fragile and vague. She looked lost. Penny appeared to be a walking zombie who had just clawed its way out of a grave.

I hugged her and held her. "Oh Penny… what has he done to you?"

She started wailing, sobbing and saying meaningless words that did not make sense. "Tommy took my baby!" she said hysterically. "My baby… my little Alec. He's gone!"

"Come in, dear sister, come in," I tried to console her but she was emotionally battered and her mind was not in a good place.

"What happened?" I said after she settled in.

Still sobbing, she stumbled through the story of how Tommy had promised them a better life in Las Vegas, sold their house and about the woman he had been hanging out with. "Honestly, I don't even care about her," said Penny. "He stole my precious Alec. I just want my baby back."

After having experienced a similar ordeal with Gus many years prior, I knew how it felt to have your child taken away from you. It felt like more than just an empty hole in your heart. It was every negative emotion ranging from hopelessness to frustration; anxiety to desperation and an unexplainable loneliness all wrapped up into one helpless ball.

I hugged her close. "Oh my little angel, you need to get away from him. He is a very evil man."

"His mother poisoned him," she said sniffing. "Things were fine until she moved here."

We talked for hours. She was my little sister and I always

felt an obligation to protect her and look out for her. I suggested that she move here to Florida. At that time she was working as a chef in a Thai restaurant near Seattle. Having finally been rewarded with the success of my real estate endeavors, I had recently purchased and opened a new convenience store. "Come work for me!" I encouraged her.

I could tell she wanted to escape the hell of Tommy's fury and her evil mother-in-law. Their money was gone and so was their house and his career with the airlines. All Penny had to do was find her child and then her life could be better away from Tommy's raging grasp and fierce control.

After visiting for a couple of weeks, Penny returned to Seattle with the intent of handling her affairs and making plans to move. I promised her I would pay for a lawyer so that she could get full custody of her son. I did not want that monster to raise my nephew, and neither did she. At that point she just wanted out of their marriage altogether.

That was the plan. However, when she returned home, Tommy was waiting for her. He lost his mind in anger that she came to visit me. Even though she was glad to be rejoined with her little boy, she was not at all glad to see her husband. There was no way he was going to let her out of his sight, ever again. Penny was his. She was his wife ... his possession. He let her know that fact repeatedly with a baseball bat to her back as she lay crumpled on the floor while their son watched, crying. "Please don't hurt Mommy," he pleaded.

Penny didn't move to Florida. She didn't dare. Tommy threatened to kill her if she ever left. In fact, he took over everything in her life and even drove her to work and picked her up at the end of the night. He knew that by managing her every move there would be no way for her to cheat on him, even though she never had.

They moved into a tiny rental house in a run-down neighborhood. Alec buried himself in schoolwork. He was abnormally bright for his age; a near genius. His grades and test results exceeded all of the other children at school. Baseball was still his greatest passion. One of his favorite players was Jamie Moyer, the left-handed pitcher who played for the Seattle Mariners. Alec often wore Jamie's signature silver and navy blue jersey with the #50 on the back to school. He dreamed of meeting him one day.

Ironically, it was these same baseball bats that Alec's father used to abuse his mother with. It seemed there was no way to escape his control. Tommy drove her to work and watched her like a hawk. He rarely let her call anyone unless he was within earshot. Meanwhile, he was gone during the day – supposedly looking for a new job. Nobody really knows if that was where he actually was. The abuse went on for another couple of years, along with continued threats and unimaginable violence.

One day, Penny broke away to call me. "I'm coming to see you," she whispered. "I'm bringing Alec."

"Are you okay?" I asked her, delicately.

"No, I'm not. I have to get out of here. Tommy is insane," she whispered. "Can we come live with you?"

"Of course!" I said. "Do you need any money? Do you want me to send you the plane tickets?"

"I'll let you know. The sooner the better," she murmured.

I reassured her. "You're going to be okay. I'll get everything ready for you. There is plenty of room and..."

"Nancy, I gotta go..." Penny said as she cut the phone visit short and hung up unexpectedly.

Those were the last words ever spoken between us.

Chapter

18

"911. PLEASE STATE YOUR EMERGENCY."

"Please, come get me." A little voice on the phone barely whispered loud enough to hear. It was about 4:00 a.m. on the night of October 22, 2004.

Dispatcher: "What's happened?"

Little boy: "My Daddy killed me with a butcher knife. Please send the army men or an ambulance."

Dispatcher: "Is he there right now?"

Little boy: "No, I think he left."

The dispatcher confirmed the name and address of 8-year old Alec Songlee. "Where is your mom?"

Alec: "She's already dead."

Dispatcher: "Are you bleeding, Alec?"

Alec: "Uh-huh."

Dispatcher: "Hang in there. Help is on the way. Where are you bleeding from?"

Alec: "My stomach. My head. Everywhere." He whimpers. "Can you hurry?"

Dispatcher: "You are going to make it. Stay with me on the phone. Tell me what happened, if you can."

Alec: "My Dad was killing my mommy. With a big knife from the kitchen. He told me to wait on the bed. Then he stabbed her a lot and said, 'You're next.' But I think I'm still alive. I kind of survived, I guess."

Dispatcher: "You're doing great Alec. Just stay on the line. What kind of car does your Dad drive?"

Alec: "A black car."

Dispatcher: "Do you know what type?"

Alec: "A Toyota, I think."

As the 911 dispatcher quickly relayed the message to a co-worker, he waved someone over to expedite the police units as fast as possible. "We're going to find him."

Alec: "I think I hear sirens."

Despite his terror, Alec didn't panic and stayed calm, answering the dispatcher's questions to the best of his ability. Unbeknownst to Alec, who lay on the floor next to his murdered mother, the police found Tommy Songlee standing in his front yard. He had blood all over his shirt and was high on methamphetamines. He didn't say a word as police ordered him to get down on the ground with his hands up. They handcuffed him and angrily stuffed him in the back of the vehicle without incident. Tommy appeared to be in a daze.

Not knowing his son was still alive, they hauled Tommy away and the paramedics rushed in to retrieve Alec. He had been stabbed six times. Penny was dead, and Alec had watched the whole thing in horror as his beloved mother was brutally killed.

Although he had to endure painful surgery of his lacerated liver, stomach and gut, Alec was lucky to be alive. His face and neck were also targeted by his angry father. His story touched the hearts of millions of Americans as the media announced his ordeal across the national news. Alec became an instant hero. He became known as the boy who called 911 and said, "My Daddy killed me."

Even though he was still physically living, in a way Alec did die a little bit that day on October 22, 2004. He lost the most important person in the world, his mother. She was everything to Alec and she was a good woman. She didn't deserve what happened to her.

After Layla called me on that dreadful day, the homicide detective and prosecutor's office sent a secret service agent to meet my husband and me in Memphis Tennessee. We had to fly there right away to help Alec, since I was the closest family he had left. Jon and I got in the car right away from our house in Florida. The timing was ironic since I had already packed a lot of things with the intent of moving out. However, those plans were placed on hold under the severity of the circumstances. Life was not about me right now. It was about my sister and nephew. Alec needed me.

Still in shock, we drove through a severe rainstorm to the airport in Tennessee. I guess they chose Nashville to throw the media off because this case created such a massive uproar across the country. People were so horrified by the monster that my sister's husband was and couldn't believe the bravery of little Alec.

As the windshield wipers swiped back and forth washing away the fierce rain, the mood was ominous. Jon reached for my hand as I stared out of the passenger side window in silence and in mourning for my sister. "She was supposed to come live with us. She was supposed to come …" I said under my breath.

"I know," was all Jon could say.

I felt like the last of my true family – except my nephew – were gone. My mother, father and sister were the only real family I knew because my older siblings had virtually disappeared when I was very little. I barely heard from them throughout my adulthood and they had no knowledge of our lives here in the United States. Nor did I know much about how their lives had fared, either.

Two men in undercover suits greeted us at a fuel station across from the airport once we reached Tennessee. To look at them, you would never have guessed them to be cops. I still didn't know the entire story about how my sister died at that point. All I knew was that she had been murdered and that my nephew was in critical condition undergoing major surgeries at the hospital in Seattle. The secret service guys escorted Jon and me to our flight. They took care of our car, as well.

I cried on the entire flight to Seattle. Penny was just too young to die. It seemed so unfair. So needless. I didn't know how bad Alec's condition was, either. It was a restless journey in the clouds to oblivion.

When we reached Seattle we were instantly escorted off the plane. A gentleman warned us that the media would be waiting. They were. We barely had enough time to step foot into the main concourse of the airport when we were surrounded by flashes, microphones and hungry media people firing questions at us left and right. I was still in shock and we didn't have any answers. This was not the kind of media attention I had ever wanted.

Somehow we made it to the hospital and were allowed to pass through. Alec was barely breathing and the doctors were waiting for us to get permission to do the necessary surgeries to repair his internal organ damage. His face and neck also needed attending. Six stab wounds were enough to have killed him. We held Alec's small hand as he lay there; just a helpless little boy who had spent most of his young life watching his own Daddy brutalize and savagely beat his mother on many occasions. It was something no child should have to experience.

After that we were escorted to the morgue where I had to positively identify my sister's body. This was one of the most difficult experiences of my life. Jon was not allowed to go in with me so I had to follow the detective on my own. When I saw what Tommy did to Penny, I was horrified beyond belief. She was barely recognizable and many of her remains were in pieces. Her awful monster of a husband had slashed her beautiful face. Dried blood smeared her eyelids like the eye shadow of a resurrection. One of her arms had a bone protruding where the elbow joins the forearm to the bicep, making it disfigured. Her mouth was ripped and gasping like a petrified yell that remained frozen upon her face. Penny's once lovely raven hair was drenched in dried up blood. Her cold and lifeless physique lay there helplessly... cold and white ... stiff.

I had never seen a dead person who looked like that. Sure, everybody has gone to a wake or a funeral of someone they know. But to experience this kind of unimaginable tragedy was painful, shocking and beyond horrifying.

How could someone do this to another human being? Why Penny? I wished I had kept her there with me when she came to visit. I wished I had reached out more and somehow saved my baby sister. At that moment when I looked down at her stabbed and dismembered body, it was the first time I felt a cold hate for another human being. Oh sure, we all have an enemy or someone we dislike, but to see the brutality staring you literally in the face is like a rude slap beyond comparison. Penny was my baby sister. How dare he! I hoped Tommy would die a horrible death and rot away like a savage in the bottom of a snake pit.

To top it off, once I learned the truth behind what had happened and the fact that Alec was made to watch his mother's horrible demise, I was even angrier. If it weren't for his bravery and pretending to die, Alec would have been yet another victim in the unfortunate and all-too-common world of domestic abuse.

In the following months after the incident, the media clamored to learn more about the miraculous tale of a boy so brave that he could pretend to die and save himself from a fierce attack. Neighbors came forward to reveal the details of that night; the frightening screams and then the strange pacing back and forth of Tommy as he stood outside of their home holding a giant butcher knife. The paramedics said there was so much blood coming from Alec's wounds that they were surprised he was still alive.

We stayed in Seattle for a total of eight months. As Alec went through the healing process, the outpouring of the community was nothing shy of amazing. Even celebrities came forward who had heard the story. Alec's idol and baseball legend Jaime Moyer even came to the hospital to see him. It was touching that so many people cared about a little boy who had spent most of his life suffering from severe domestic abuse. Of course we filed for custody of Alec but there were others who wanted to adopt him, including many celebrities. They already had eight children so adding Alec to the mix was not a problem. Even though I was gracious to them for their offer, I told them we would be able to raise Alec in honor of my sister and that I thought it was best for him to stay with someone in the family. Even though I could never replace a true mother's love for her son, my own love for Alec was the next best thing because my sister and I were very close.

There were other big celebrities who took an interest in Alec's story. We had media in our faces constantly, especially as the prosecutor began the proceedings for Tommy's trial. Oprah Winfrey invited Alec and our family to her show. Even the paramedics and the wonderful 911 operator were there. The headlines read; "The Heart of a Giant Can Live in the Tiniest of Bodies".

It was so true, Alec was a hero. He was featured in a book and on every major network. ABC, CBS, CNN, FOX and others. Jon and I were exhausted from talking to the media every day. It was ironic in a way, that I had spent most of my life wishing to be in the limelight and now finally I had a chance to rub elbows with the celebrities I had admired, but it was not for the greater good. Evil had inflicted itself upon my family and now Alec and I had become the face of our family's honor.

As the court date inched closer, I dreaded having to face my sister's murderer. What he had done was so horrific that I hoped he would get the death penalty.

Instead, Tommy surprised all of us by confronting his own actions. Once in front of the judge, he pled guilty for his actions in order to spare Alec the pain of enduring a trial and having to face his father.

"I just want to say, I'm sorry for everything. I'm sorry

to my son and to my wife's family who lost a loved one. I regret what I did and take full responsibility for my actions," Songlee told the judge.

"Why did you do this?" I yelled from my seat.

Even though he didn't have to answer, Tommy claimed he was possessed by evil spirits and that a demon told him to kill his family. "It was the spirit of my abusive stepfather. He told me to do it. He made me do it."

We knew better. It was the drug induced rage and hatred for my sister that brought Tommy to murder. Drugs in the wrong hands equal disastrous and tragic measurements. However this was only the pinnacle of what had been years of malicious and unbearable horrors for Penny.

"I want to spare my son the pain of having to relive that awful night," Tommy said to the judge. "He's my only son and ... I'm sorry ... I'm just sorry."

With that, Tommy hung his head in shame. The judge had little pity for him as she listened to his pathetic excuse, although everyone in the courtroom was relieved that he seized accountability for his actions. Nothing could ever replace my sister's life, no matter how harsh or lenient the sentence would be.

The judge sentenced Tommy to 28 years in prison. To me this didn't seem like a severe enough punishment. In fact, Alec would still be a young man at the age of 36 if his father served the entire sentence. In my eyes I felt as though he should have been locked away permanently.

THE QUEST FOR SERENDIPITY

As we left the courtroom with Alec, we were met once again by the media on the steps outside. They surrounded us with microphones and flashes. The hungry paparazzi were all scrambling to get a quote for the evening news. "How do you feel about the sentence, Mrs. Wakely?" someone yelled.

"Do you think there's a chance that Alec will want to see his father again one day to ask him, 'WHY?'" yelled another.

"How is Alec doing right now?" said another nosy reporter. "Is this affecting his abilities to go to school or play baseball?"

Jon piped in to answer for us, since both Alec and I were overwhelmed and shaken by the sight of seeing Tommy in person again. "We think the sentence is in Alec's best interest," Jon stated. "And Alec is handling the whole thing really well. He's doing great in school just like he always has. He continues to love baseball and plays nearly year-round."

After that, most of our affairs in Seattle were nearly finished. Of course another judge granted Jon and me the full custody of Alec at another civil hearing not long thereafter. We were all relieved that the horrible events were finally moving behind us. The next hurdle was the move back to Florida.

Throughout our journey to Seattle, my faithful business partner back home handled all of my affairs. I was thankful for Henry's help and somehow still managed to come out on top despite the horrific events that we had witnessed and endured.

Even though Alec was disappointed to leave his friends

and favorite baseball team behind in Washington, he handled the transition well and even looked forward to the move to Florida. Alec had become somewhat of a celebrity in his own right, just by surviving.

He attributed his survival to angels lifting him and staying with him throughout that night. "God helped me and sent an angel," said Alec. "The angel carried me to the phone so I could call 911." Alec said the voice told him to play dead until his father left the house, even as he lay there bleeding from his head, neck, back and mid-section.

Meanwhile, I talked with him about his mother and told him about all of the great memories I shared with her. Alec seemed to like hearing those stories about his mother and me when we were young. It was soothing and comforting to him. He said he thought about her every day.

After Alec lived with us for a couple of months, he started having frequent nightmares and spooks. He sometimes still hides in the closet on those nights when the memories and terror of his ordeal get the better of him, even though he knows that his father is behind bars.

The Seattle Mariners invited Alec back to their stadium as a celebrity guest. He was allowed the honor of throwing the first pitch, which had always been a lifelong dream. The team told us it was an honor to help boost the spirits of a little boy who's been through such a horrific tragedy. For many people who have heard his story, Alec brings inspiration and courage.

THE QUEST FOR SERENDIPITY

For me, Alec brought the needed distraction and gratitude that the rest of my family did not offer. I felt for the first time in a long time that someone appreciated me and needed me for more than just money, presents or a place to live. Alec was just happy to be alive and to have someone who cared about him. To me, that was worth everything.

Chapter

19

I T WAS EXCITING MEETING OPRAH WINFREY,
even though the circumstances brought forth many
mixed feelings regarding the tragic events of my sister's
death. To me, Oprah represents everything I have hoped of
becoming. Like me, she was a minority born into difficult
circumstances, but she never let the suffering of childhood
poverty deter her from moving forth into a world of success.

I feel like I can relate to Oprah on many levels. Apparently
she was so poor she had to wear potato sacks as dresses and
the local kids often ridiculed her attire. I too, was scorned
sometimes for the clothing I wore. Oprah was taught to read at
the age of three by her grandmother, who also instilled strong
faith by making her learn biblical verses even at a very early
age. She also endured unforeseen hardships as a teen and
was sent to live with the man she believed to be her biological
father. He was strict, coming from a background in the army
but it was because of him that she made the honor roll and
achieved a scholarship to the Tennessee State University.

Like me, Oprah also entered beauty pageants and she

won Miss Black Tennessee. She strived to better herself and became one of the richest and most famous women in America. So meeting her was more than just an honor, it was an inspiration. I felt like she and I had so many qualities that were shared. Although my circumstances were on a much smaller scale, the dire poverty to subsequent success we both achieved was a characteristic I could empathize with.

Occasionally the paparazzi still come by to ask questions about my nephew, but for the most part the ordeal with my sister's tragic murder have become lost in the memories of the public. There are new murders and other tragic occurrences every day. It is a wonder if anyone can keep up with all of them.

Unfortunately the whole ordeal made it less possible for me to leave Jon. For my nephew's sake I was not able to get divorced because the child protective services made us prove that we had a good home to raise him, especially since Alec had already endured the emotional and physical pain of domestic abuse. Jon was never abusive in that way. He was just not a good provider financially. However, the kids always loved him and underneath it all Jon has a good heart. Lack of ambition doesn't necessarily make someone a bad spouse unless the other spouse sees it that way. I still wish Jon would go out and do something wonderful instead of counting on me to be the breadwinner.

Alec adjusted very well to his new home. I enrolled him with a therapist so that he could talk about the loss of his mother. It would be so unfortunate for him to think that all men were like his father, but Alec is very smart and knows that his father was a monster in every sense of the word. He was a sick man who did not deserve to have children. Nevertheless, Alec is one of life's biggest blessings and he is nothing short of a childhood genius.

By the age of 14 he had already received his high school diploma and received acceptance letters to several colleges. He planned on playing baseball. To this day, Alec's future is bright. There is no doubt that he was meant to live. By his account, Alec has told us that an angel helped him through the situation. As his father was murdering his mother and then turned on him, an angel told him to be still and play dead.

Then the angel carried him to the phone and helped him talk to the 911 dispatcher, even as the blood from his tiny body continued gushing and soaking into his hair and clothing, covering him from head to toe. The angel told him not to fear and that she would keep him alive. That is why Alec is here to this day.

To this day, Alec is still an avid Mariners fan. Alec wants to be a famous baseball player someday. I believe that with his tenacious and driven spirit and will to live; he will become anything he wants to be.

It turns out, Alec's favorite baseball player for the Mariners is a diehard advocates of children and has raised millions of dollars to support children who are grieving the loss of family members or friends. The Moyer Foundation is the largest network of bereavement camps through a nationwide 'Campaign for Kids' that now has camps in over 60 cities across America.

As for Jon and I, our strained relationship has become more of a friendship or tolerance of one another. We sold our house in the Pan Handle and live in San Antonio full time, where I now have a successful jewelry store called 'Thai Princess Jewelry' that attracts many locals and tourists to the lovely Riverwalk in downtown San Antonio, Texas. Each year millions of tourists come to the Riverwalk and take boat tours or enjoy shopping and other activities of bustling San Antonio.

Meanwhile, I still enjoy investing with my business partner and dear friend, Henry. We have many successful endeavors that lie before us and the future looks promising.

People ask me every day, "What do you do to be so successful?" Many of them do not know of the countless hardships I have endured to get here. They just see the beautiful jewelry or the beautiful home and car and think that I stepped on wealth accidentally, when in fact I still work at becoming better and even more successful every day. It is my utmost wish to share with everyone who asks, the answer to my quest for success is not happenstance. It is resilience.

Every day I pray. I stick a note on my mirror every day that is my source of inspiration. On the note I see my goals in front of me, staring at my reflection. The note says; "This is what I will do today to be successful…" and then I write down the things I need to achieve each day. It is by living every day and embracing every moment head on, rather than worrying so much about next week, next month or next year, that I am able to accomplish and handle everything that life dishes.

Just like everyone else who may be reading my story, I still have plenty of setbacks. Some days I feel misguided by those who may have ulterior motives, yet I give everybody the benefit of the doubt. I never let the setbacks become obsessions and rarely dwell on anything that is negative. Instead, I just keep moving forward.

Setting a goal every day is the trick to accomplishment. Writing down a number of what you want to earn or who you want to inspire, or something you want to overcome. I hope everyone reading this will try my strategy. Through prayer and gratitude there is nothing that cannot be accomplished.

Even if there is no money coming in and things seem desperate, by remaining faithful and hopeful it always has a way of working out. Sometimes I have stayed up until 2:00 in the morning to meet my goal for the day. Rather than just sitting and waiting for things to happen, you just have to go after it. Instead of complaining about what isn't there, you have to ignore the setbacks and reach for what is there, even if it has yet to be seen.

Whether you believe in God, Buddha, the Universe or a higher source, it is important to believe in something. People these days thrive on hating each other for the belief they do not understand. But everyone is raised from a different background. With so many mixed countries, cultures, religions and multitudes of diversity it is important that we understand and unite as humans; not as one race over another. I say if someone believes in God that is great. If someone believes in Buddha, that is great too. These seeming divides of cultural diversity have brought the world farther apart, when in fact the fundamental source of being is really the same.

We are blessed to be alive. Everyone endures hardship through life in some way. It's just much worse for some than others. I have a soft spot in my heart for children, especially those who are born into undesirable circumstances. However, when I do get a chance to say something or inspire a child I tell them that no matter how bad it is right now, one day life can be great. You can be successful.

I feel grateful to have had the opportunity to fulfill the dreams that I've held on to since childhood. Despite so many adversities it was those dreams that kept me going. Now I finally can afford housekeeping and live in my own mansion, after living in a simple shack and sleeping on musty straw beds. Not only have I overcome all of these would-be setbacks, I still have many dreams yet to fulfill.

If it weren't for those angels I have met along my journey, I would not be where I am right now. Angels like Pete, the man who lifted me up out of the rain after I was raped and who cared for me in the months that followed after I ran away from home. Angels like Anna, who helped me care for my children after my husband moved to Colorado and deserted our family. Angles like Henry, who believed in me and agreed to go into business with a woman who had terrible credit but plenty of wonderful ideas and ambition. Angels like Alec, my beautiful nephew who helped me to realize the true value of life and who inspired the whole country with his amazing human spirit and courage to live.

Angels come in many forms and are not always just heavenly or spiritual. Angels could be me, or you. When you make a difference to someone else who is worse off than you are, then you can also become an angel to them. There are millions of angels among us; some whom we have yet to meet.

Through this autobiography it is my new goal to make other women feel empowered, especially those who have gone through a terrible relationship. Abuse comes in many forms. Some women endure emotional abuse instead of physical, which can be equally damaging. Children, too. It's such a shame when the innocence of a child is lost by the betrayal of an elder.

I do finally have someone special who loves me, even if it might be taboo. With both of my husbands I have experienced the pain of rejection by my in-laws because of my skin color and upbringing. However, true love does not look at the color of skin nor the background for which someone is raised. These are things that people fundamentally have no control over. Whether that person has a good heart and is a good person should be the values that are embraced by our society.

THE QUEST FOR SERENDIPITY

Imagine if you were in a car accident and there was no one there to help you. Suddenly someone appears. What if that person was of a skin color you have ever ridiculed or rejected? Would you still want their help? Would you be worth saving? What if that person decided to leave you there to die just because you were of a different background, religion, color or even sexual preference?

Because I have felt and seen the hate for much of my adulthood, I choose to love instead. That is the difference between becoming successful or struggling through life. Once people embrace the love, they too can become happy and successful just as I have. They can accomplish more, love more, and be free of society's expectations. By living to bring joy to others is always the ultimate way to bring joy into your own life.

There are still many things I want to accomplish and qualities I want to work on regarding my own set of values. I want other women who feel afraid to take a stand against their attackers. We all have made excuses for enduring undesirable living circumstances, but those few who have made the decision to change often feel a great ocean of relief afterwards. Understandably, this is much easier said than done. Just know that it can be done if you go after it. Happiness is there for everyone who makes a decision to embrace it.

ACKNOWLEDGEMENTS

I would like to give a special notation of gratitude to the following individuals and organizations:

First of all, to my family who believed in me all of these years. I love you all.

To my awesome writer Anne Violette, I so enjoyed working with you. I have wanted to get my story out for so long and you finally made it come to fruition with your beautiful words. I couldn't have done it without you and your wonderful advice. I'm glad we became good friends and look forward to writing many more books together.

Henry, I want to thank you for supporting me throughout the years and for introducing me to the real me, the one who was destined to become successful. You are my inspiration.

To Historical Publishing Network, I look forward to our imminent success.

Of course I must give tremendous gratitude to my "angel investors" who are worthy of the name angels. They are the people who believed in me and lent money to me over the years for my business endeavors. I would never have been able to get off the ground and finally realize success without your backing.

Thanking D.P. Janssen and Darrell is an absolute must, especially during the difficult time with my mother in the hospital. Thank you so much. You were my rock and support system and remain such true friends to this very day.

To Heidi my photographer, thanks for making me look good!

I must say thank you to James Timothy White for introducing me to my writer and also for being a good friend. You always make me laugh.

My new assistant Joemar has been especially helpful with audio-visual activities and so far, I am very pleased in his abilities.

Rose Zamora, I so greatly appreciate your ongoing legal advice. You never steer me wrong. Thank you. You're the best!

Without Anne E. I would have never learned about "The Millionaire Mind." You are the one who introduced me to the wealth mindset and I would never have known how to invest my money had it not been for you.

Then there are all of those friends who have believed in me over the years; you know who you are. The ones who never doubted me and always knew I could become successful. I remained on course due to your faith in me and appreciate those close friendships I have acquired along my life's travels.

Made in the USA
San Bernardino, CA
09 May 2015